# WATER FEATURES
## FOR THE GARDEN

# WATER FEATURES
## FOR THE GARDEN
### Including 16 easy-to-build projects

## ALAN & GILL BRIDGEWATER

NEW
HOLLAND

First published in 2001 by New Holland Publishers (UK) Ltd
London • Cape Town • Sydney • Auckland

24 Nutford Place, London W1H 6DQ, United Kingdom

80 McKenzie Street, Cape Town, 8001, South Africa

Level 1, Unit 4, 14 Aquatic Drive, Frenchs Forest, NSW 2086, Australia

Unit 1A, 218 Lake Road, Northcote, Auckland

ISBN 1 85974 441 9

Editorial direction: Rosemary Wilkinson
Project editor: Kate Latham
Production: Caroline Hansell

Designed and created for New Holland by AG&G BOOKS
Design: Glyn Bridgewater
Illustrators: Alan and Gill Bridgewater
Project design: Alan and Gill Bridgewater
Photography: Ian Parsons unless otherwise credited (see page 128)
Editor: Fiona Corbridge
Project makers: Alan, Gill and Glyn Bridgewater

Reproduction by Modern Age Repro House Ltd, Hong Kong
Printed and bound in Malaysia by Times Offset (M) Sdn. Bhd.

# Contents

# Introduction

**W**e both enjoy working with water. When we were first married and living in a country cottage, we always liked using the well and messing about with various hand- and wind-driven pumps. Later on, when we began working with wood, stone and garden design, we soon came to realize that water is a uniquely beguiling element. We discovered that building, stocking and maintaining small ponds, from digging the hole to fitting the liner, choosing plants, and getting the pump working, is great fun.

The ambition of this book is to share with you all the pure "playtime" pleasures of working with wood, brick, earth and stone to create water features in the garden. Each project progresses through design considerations to instructions on how to use the tools and materials, how to fit pumps and fountains, and ideas on modifying the projects to suit your individual needs. Colour-wash illustrations show how the structures are put together, and step-by-step photographs illustrate the procedures involved – providing a complete tour through all the stages of designing, making, constructing and finishing. And after the pleasure of building a water feature, you can "soak up" the calming effect of water.

Making water features does not require complex tools or a profound knowledge of earth and pump mechanics, only that you become involved in the exciting and therapeutic experience of working with water – our most precious resource, and one of our most tantalizing natural elements. This book is about working with your hands in the garden, and using your mind and body to create uniquely beautiful water features that everyone can enjoy, both for their visual impact and as a relaxing experience.

So – best of luck!

*Alan & Gill*

---

**HEALTH AND SAFETY**

*Many of the procedures for making water features are potentially dangerous, so before starting the projects, check through the following list:*

- The projects use safe low-voltage water pumps, but we still recommend using a safety electricity circuit breaker (between the power socket and the plug for the pump), and armoured pipe to protect the power cable. If you are unsure about installing the pumps, ask a qualified electrician to fit them for you.
- Some projects are physically demanding and if you have doubts about whether you are up to

it, get advice from your doctor. When lifting large weights, minimize back strain by bending your knees, hugging the item close to your body, and keeping the spine straight.
- Have a first-aid kit and telephone within easy reach. If possible, avoid working alone.
- Wear gloves, dust-mask and goggles when you are handling cement and lime.
- We recommend that you do not build a pond in your garden if you have small children. A toddler can drown in less than 10 mm of water. Other water features are safer, but even so, never leave children unsupervised.

# Part I: Techniques

# Designing and planning

Size doesn't matter! Whether you have a town courtyard or a big country garden, a pond, fountain or other water feature can be accommodated in any size of garden. The secret of building a successful water feature is to spend time carefully designing and planning the whole operation, from walking around the garden and choosing the site, to tidying up when the job is done. This attention to detail guarantees that the end results will be impressive.

## FIRST CONSIDERATIONS

- Do you want to involve yourself in a lot of earth-moving, or would you prefer to minimize the digging and build a feature that sits on the ground?
- Do you want a low-cost water feature with a short life, or would it be better to build something that is more expensive but is going to be around for the next 25 years?
- Do small children and pets use your garden?
- Do you want lots of movement and sound – perhaps a small pool with a gushing fountain? Or would you prefer a large, natural pond with abundant plants and wildlife?
- Where and how are you going to hide the water feed and the power cable? Where is the nearest power source?
- Do you want a water feature with minimum maintenance? Or can you cope with lots of work, such as raking leaves out of a pond, adjusting the pumps, and stocking it with plants and fish?
- Are you going to start work in the summer when the ground is dry? If so, can you put up with the upheaval at a time when you are most likely to want to sit out in the garden? Or are you going to work in winter, so that you can appreciate the water feature at the start of the gardening year in the spring?

## Choosing the right project

When you have worked through the First Considerations, decide precisely what you want to build, and where in the garden you are going to put it. This involves looking at the land and thinking about the implications of the operations. Let's say, for example, that you want to build the Natural Pond (page 118). The garden is big enough, and you are not put off by all the digging, but where are you going to put the excavated earth? Of course you could pay to have it removed, but why not leave the mound of earth alongside the pond and build a waterfall cascade, or a rockery. If the excavated earth is going to be a problem, it may be better to opt for another project such as the Woodland Grotto (page 88), or perhaps a fountain. You have to assess each project according to your own requirements. You also need to consider how a project affects other members of the household, including safety considerations for young children, and whether it will be a nuisance to neighbours in any way.

## Planning the project

The whole project now has to be planned out in the context of your garden. Decide where you want the water feature to be placed in relation to existing garden features, and measure out the distances for the various cables and pipes.

Next, you have to think about the delivery of materials for the project, and the way the movement of those materials is going to affect the everyday use of the garden. For example, if you are going to order a tonne of sand, and you need to dig a trench across the lawn and under a path, you have to consider all the implications. Where can the sand be unloaded? How is an open trench going to affect your passage across the garden? Sit down and write out the order of operations, and work out the details.

Measure your garden and do a rough sketch showing the position and size of the envisaged project. This will give you a good idea of how it relates to other features. Before you start digging up the garden and ordering materials, it's a good idea to do a final check to make sure that the scale of the project is just right. The best way to do this is to set out the dimensions of the project on the ground with pegs and string, and then to cover the site with a large tarpaulin. Live with this object for a few days, and if, at the end of that time, the size is just too much, or you reckon that the intended pond could be a bit larger, or you have spotted a problem concerning the pipework, you can make changes.

Last but not least, you need to draw up a schedule of work, to see if things such as local events and holidays affect your dates. For example, it is no good planning to do a project over a public holiday, if this is when you want suppliers to deliver materials.

## Buying the right tools and materials

Though the tools and materials will depend upon your chosen project, there are two guiding principles: it is always wise to purchase the best tools that you can afford, and it is always less expensive to buy materials in bulk. Of course, you could trim costs slightly by making do with your spade for shovelling sand and gravel, rather than getting a shovel, and you can cut down on the thickness of sand under a plastic liner, but consider the implications. Is the wear and tear on your back worth the saving on the shovel? Is the meagre saving on sand going to result in the expensive pond liner being pierced? Do not cut costs at the expense of the success of your project. Consider hiring items such as angle grinders and large drills, rather than buying them.

# WATER FEATURE DESIGNS FOR THE GARDEN

*Weeping hypertufa boulder*
*A unique and intriguing water feature that is best placed in a quiet area of the garden*

*Rocky cascade*
*Positioned in a secluded corner so that the sight and sound of falling water can be appreciated*

*Wall mask waterspout*
*Built against a wall, this is the perfect feature for an old house and garden*

*Japanese deer scarer*
*Placed next to a natural pond*

*Natural pond*
*The perfect habitat for natural fauna: fish, frogs and newts*

*Glass waterfall*
*A chance to get high-tech – also a great feature for courtyard gardens*

*Romantic fountain*
*Positioned so that it can be seen from a seating area*

*Container bog garden*
*A quick and easy way to bring the garden closer to the house*

*Copper cascade*
*Set beside a pond – a beautiful feature using contrasting materials*

*Mini marble fountain*
*A perfect feature for a sun lounge*

*French millstone bell fountain*
*For best effect, set this fountain in an area of flat lawn*

*Still pond*
*Built close to the house so it can be seen from indoors as the rain falls*

*Perpetual water tap*
*A water feature that will entertain children and friends*

*Copper spiral spray*
*Set in a courtyard, the copper spiral catches the breeze as well as the trickling water*

*Wine bottle spray fountain*
*Positioned near a patio seating area so that family and friends can admire it*

*Woodland grotto*
*Turns the bottom of your garden into an enchanted wonderland – and a favourite spot for toads*

ABOVE **The sight and sound of water is truly uplifting. Building a water feature, and then sitting back and looking at your handiwork, are both equally enjoyable experiences. The garden design above demonstrates how the projects in this book might be arranged.**

# Tools

**Using the correct tools makes all the difference to the ease and speed with which you can complete a project. If a tool is too short or the wrong weight, you may get backache, but if it is the right length and well designed, you get the job done more quickly and with less stress. A well-chosen, quality tool is a worthwhile investment.**

## TOOLS FOR MOVING MATERIALS

*Wheelbarrow*

*Gloves*

*Bucket*

### Protecting your feet and hands

You must wear solid workboots, preferably with steel toecaps, to prevent your feet from getting crushed. Gloves might feel a little unmanageable in the first instance, but they will stop your hands getting abraded and otherwise damaged. Digging, lifting buckets, heaving concrete slabs, and mixing sand and cement are all hard on the hands. It's a good idea to have several pairs of gloves: leather for the general work, and rubber for the watery tasks.

### Making the work easier

Of all the lifting and carrying tools, it is the wheelbarrow and the bucket that make life easier. The best type of wheelbarrow is one with a large inflated rubber tyre that allows you to bounce your way up slopes and over steps, and a tip-stop bar in front of the wheel that enables you to bring the barrow to a halt and tip out the load. You also need three or four plastic buckets. Get the cheapest you can find and use them until they fall to bits.

## TOOLS FOR MEASURING AND MARKING

*Spirit level*

*Tape measure*

### Measuring

Ideally, you need two measuring tools – a flexible tape measure for setting out the site plan, and a measuring rule for smaller measuring tasks within the project. Make sure that both tools are marked out in metric and imperial, so that you can deal with products that are described in either system. It is also a good idea to get a fibreglass tape measure, which is unaffected by water, whereas a metal tape soon rusts if it gets wet. When you are measuring, follow the old adage "measure twice and cut once" – meaning (in this context) it is much better to double-check at the measuring stage, before you start doing clever things such as digging incorrectly-sized holes in the wrong position.

### Marking out

You need four marking-out tools – wooden pegs and string, a thick rope, a piece of chalk and a spirit level. The wooden pegs and string are used for marking boundaries and for scribing circles. The rope maps out large, irregular shapes, such as the Natural Pond (page 118). Buy a type that resists tangling. The chalk is used for drawing on concrete and wood when you need a broad, general mark, rather than for making a precise measurement. Lastly, you need a spirit level for checking horizontal and vertical levels. Buy the best that you can afford, preferably one with a strong aluminum body and shock-proof spirit phials. Look after your spirit level, and try not to drop it.

# TOOLS FOR PREPARING A SITE

*Spade*

*Shovel*

*Fork*

*Garden rake*

*Lawn rake*

*Garden trowel*

### Removing turf and digging earth

A spade and shovel deal with the tasks of removing turf and digging earth. Mark out the size of the pond or water feature, take the spade and cut down through the thickness of the turf. Slice it into easy-to-manage squares, lift these into a wheelbarrow, and unload them off-site. Finally, use both the spade and the shovel to excavate the earth to the required depth.

### Compacting hardcore and raking

A club hammer makes short work of compacting hardcore. The smaller the stones of the hardcore, the easier it is to compact. Builder's rubble requires a lot of effort, while gravel settles under its own weight. Avoid rubble that contains lumps of concrete, as they are very difficult to break up. Spread your chosen material over the area and pound it into place with a club hammer.

Use a fork for moving clumps of earth, a garden rake for spreading earth and shingle, a lawn rake for spreading sand and for tidying up and a garden trowel for small excavations. Try to choose tool sizes that match your body size.

### Mixing cement and moving gravel

The simplest way of mixing loose material – such as cement, sand and gravel – is to use a carefully chosen shovel. Ideally, you need a tool of a weight and handle length to suit your height and strength. If you are not sure which to buy, always select the shovel with the longest handle. Wash the shovel after mixing cement. Never try shovelling with a spade or digging with a shovel – both exercises are a back-breaking waste of time! Use a wheelbarrow if you need to move the material from one part of the garden to another, even if it's only a few strides away.

## MASONRY TOOLS

*Mason's hammer*

*Club hammer*

*Cold chisel*

### Cutting concrete, stone, brick and mortar

At various times, you will need to cut a piece of stone or a concrete slab, rake out an existing mortar joint, or generally cut and break hard materials. A club hammer and cold chisel are good for chopping stone to size and for cutting holes in brickwork, while a mason's hammer (also known as a brick hammer) can be used for everything from nipping stone to shape, to banging in wooden pegs, and generally excavating holes in hard and rocky earth. The quality of the tools you buy should depend on whether or not you want them to last for many years or not. For example, an inexpensive chisel will soon lose its edge, but you might well decide that it only needs to last the length of the project. But if a "bargain" tool is going to make life difficult, you do have to consider the wear and tear on your patience.

## CUTTING WOOD, PLASTIC AND METAL

*Log saw*

*Scissors*

*Craft knife*

*Coping saw*

*Metal snips*

*Pipe cutter*

### Wood

Generally, most projects can be managed with the log saw, which is perfect for cutting railway sleepers and large-section sawn wood. However, a coping saw is necessary for making the Japanese Deer Scarer featured on page 68. Make sure that both saws have spare blades, so the project will not be held up if a blade breaks.

### Plastic

You will need a strong pair of scissors for cutting plastic sheet and the various soft plastic pipes, and a knife for all manner of cutting and whittling tasks. However, you can use the log saw for cutting plastic rainwater pipe and wire snips for some of the water delivery hoses. Some suppliers will cut plastics to specific sizes.

### Metal

Metal snips can be used for just about everything from cutting metal and mesh through to cutting some of the tougher plastics, and one or two other tasks besides. Another very useful tool is the pipe cutter, which is a plumbing tool. It is wonderfully easy to use: you simply hook it on the copper pipe, tighten up the single turn-screw, and spin the tool around the pipe until the three wheels cut through the copper. This beautifully designed and inexpensive tool makes a perfect cut every time, without making ragged edges or deforming the pipe. It gives a crisp, cut edge that is set at right angles to the run of the pipe. When you buy the pipe cutter, make sure that it comes with a couple of spare cutting wheels, a mini screwdriver, and instructions for use.

## TOOLS FOR CONCRETE, MORTAR AND HYPERTUFA

*Bricklayer's trowel*

*Pointing trowel*

*Mortar float*

### Spreading concrete and mortar

If you want to spread concrete or mortar to a smooth finish, you need to use a tool called a mortar float. Made from steel, wood or plastic, the tool is used with an even, side-to-side skimming and smoothing action – in much the same way as you use a bricklayer's trowel. After use, it is vital to wash the float to remove all traces of cement. Never wash your tools at the kitchen sink, as the fine sludge will block up pipes and drains.

### Handling mortar

The bricklayer's trowel is designed specifically for transferring large slaps of mortar from where it is mixed to the workpiece. The pointing trowel is for pointing brickwork and more detailed work, but many beginners prefer to use the smaller pointing trowel for all tasks. If you are a novice, use whichever tool you prefer. It is best to avoid the all-plastic trowels and spatulas that are coming onto the market, because they are not as strong.

## OTHER ESSENTIAL TOOLS

*Drill bit for wood and metal*

*Flat screwdriver*

*Electric drill*

*Adjustable spanner*

*Cross-point screwdriver*

*Claw hammer*

*Paintbrush*

### Drilling holes

Many of the projects require you to drill holes. Use an electric drill fitted with the appropriate twist bit for drilling holes in sheet metal, plastic, wood and concrete. Always fit an electricity circuit breaker if you are using an electric drill out in the garden, especially when you are working near water. For drilling very small holes that need to be very accurately placed, use a hand drill. For drilling holes through railway sleepers, we prefer to use a carpenter's brace, fitted with a long auger bit.

### Tightening up screws and bolts

Many different screw and bolt fixings are used on water features, such as slot-headed and cross-headed wood screws, screw-bolts on hose fittings, slot-headed machine screws in the pumps, and all manner of hex nuts and bolts. Ideally, you need a whole range of screwdrivers and a single top-quality adjustable spanner or

wrench to deal with all these. Many of the hose clips and pumps have fixings that need to be tightened up with a key, but such tools are usually supplied with the product. If you are a beginner – meaning you are starting without a tool kit – it is best to buy the materials first and then get the appropriate tools to fit.

### Back-up tools

You will need a whole range of non-specific back-up tools, such as a claw hammer for driving in nails, brushes and various electricity circuit breakers. As such tools can be used generally about the house and garden, it is a good idea to get the best-quality tools that you can afford. As a general rule of thumb, we think it fair to say that tools made by long-established British, American, Swedish and German firms – especially forged metal tools, such as hammers and drills – are many times better than those made in developing countries. Be warned – there are no bargains!

# Materials

**The materials come from four main sources: a general builder's merchant for items such as sand and cement, a specialist supplier for bulk items such as shingle and topsoil, a garden centre for concrete slabs and plants, and a water garden specialist for plastic sheet, pumps and fountains. Always shop around for the best prices.**

## SUMPS, PIPES, INSULATION AND LINERS

*Sump*

*Reinforced garden hosepipe*

*Clear plastic pipe*

*Green plastic pipe*

*Flexible armoured pipe*

*Loft insulation*

*Plastic sheet*     *Thin PVC liner*     *Thick butyl liner*

### Sumps

A sump, sometimes known as a sump reservoir, or even just a reservoir, is a smallish, bucket-sized container which is sunk into the ground, where it is used to hold just enough water to feed a pump. The pump sits in the sump, pushing water up and out, which then falls to be channelled back into the sump, and so on.

Such an arrangement is ideal when you want to create a feature with moving water, without going to the trouble of building a pool. You can either opt for a self-contained, purpose-built plastic sump that comes complete with its own drainage brim and lid, or you can simply set a plastic bucket in the ground and cover it with a large sheet of plastic (with a slit in it) that directs all the water back into the bucket. If you do decide to use a bucket, remove the handle so that it will not pierce the plastic sheet.

### Plastic pipes

Plastic pipes are used to conduct water and protect electric cables. We use large-diameter ribbed pipe, also called armoured pipe, for large-flow delivery, such as for running water from a pond to the top of a cascade. Other gauges of plastic pipe are employed for general pump-to-pipe linkage and for cable protection. All the projects in this book use low-voltage pumps in conjunction with an electricity circuit breaker, and we protect the electric cables variously with best-quality armoured pipe and offcuts of ribbed water delivery hose. When you are working with plastic pipe, using it for water delivery or for linking a pump, be careful not to kink the pipe because it will reduce or cut off the water flow. Try to arrange it in broad, smooth curves.

## Lining material

Pond liners are generally made either from black PVC or black butyl rubber. The quality and thickness of the liner relates directly to its durability, so the thicker the liner, the longer it is going to last. At one end of the price scale there is inexpensive, thin PVC sheet that lasts approximately five years, through to very expensive, thick butyl sheet that is guaranteed to last at least 25 years. The thicker, more expensive liners are less prone to sunlight deterioration, accidental tearing and puncturing. Always

protect your chosen liner by bedding it on a layer of sand, fibreglass loft insulation or special polyester matting. As a general rule, you should avoid walking over a pond liner. That said, if you do have to walk over the liner, make sure that you wear smooth, soft-soled shoes, so that you don't make holes.

## Calculating the size of the liner

There are various formulas for calculating the size of the pond liner needed for a project, but we generally work it out by adding three times the depth of the pond to both its finished length and width. For example, if the pond is 3 metres long, 2 metres wide and 1 metre deep, you would add 3 metres to both the length and width, giving a measurement of 6 metres long by 5 metres wide. However, the simplest way to calculate liner size is to dig the hole and run a tape measure from one end down into the hole, and up out of the other side, to calculate the length (and the same for the width). Add about 30 mm to each measurement for an overlap. If in doubt, it is better to buy too big, rather than too small.

## COPPER PIPE AND SHEET, PIPE JOINTS AND FIXINGS

*Hose clip*

*Cross-headed and slot-headed screws*

*Coach bolt*

*Compression joint*

*Pipe bracket*

*Copper plumbing pipe*

*Flexible copper pipe*

*Copper sheet*

## Copper pipe and sheet

If you want to have metal on show in the garden, copper is a good choice. Not only is it relatively easy to cut and bend, but it weathers to an attractive blue-green verdigris finish.

We use hard copper pipe (15 mm in diameter) in conjunction with compression joints and pipe brackets for runs from straight to right angle, flexible copper pipe (10 mm in diameter) for bending into more complex curves, and copper sheet for simple constructions. Copper can be softened and coloured simply by using a blowlamp to heat it until it turns cherry red, then dunking it in cold water – at which point it becomes soft enough to bend, and a beautiful dappled bronze colour.

## Fixings and pipe joints

The projects all use a range of basic DIY fixings – everything from screws and nails through to coach bolts and patent hose clips. Hose clips are particularly useful when it comes to joining various sizes of pipe to the pump. It is best to purchase a mixed bag of different-sized hose clips, and then pick them to suit the project.

The simplest method of joining two lengths of copper pipe is to use an item known as a compression joint. You simply cut the pipes to length, push the ends in your chosen joint (which can be straight, right-angled, or T-junction) and then tighten them up with a spanner. Such joints can be clenched quite easily – it takes no more effort than turning off a stiff tap.

## STONE, BRICKS AND PAVING SLABS, SAND, CEMENT AND LIME

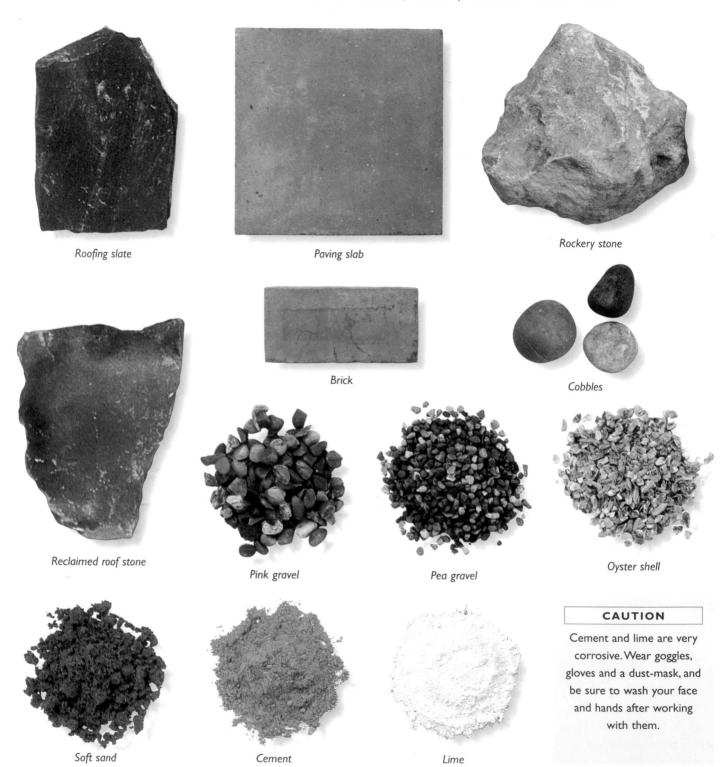

Roofing slate

Paving slab

Rockery stone

Brick

Cobbles

Reclaimed roof stone

Pink gravel

Pea gravel

Oyster shell

Soft sand

Cement

Lime

### CAUTION

Cement and lime are very corrosive. Wear goggles, gloves and a dust-mask, and be sure to wash your face and hands after working with them.

### Stone

The projects feature roofing slate, reclaimed roof stone, rockery stone in the form of limestone and split sandstone, cobbles and different types and grades of shingle and gravel. Slate and sandstone provide sheet material, limestone is good when you want rugged lumps and boulders, and cobbles and gravel are suitable for spreading over large areas. Although the projects describe specific stones, you can buy the type that most closely matches these recommendations, according to what is available in your area. If you only need a relatively small quantity of something – say a couple of bags – then it is simplest to buy it from a builder's merchant. For large amounts (as with the stone used for the Rocky Cascade on page 112), the most economical option is to order the stone directly from a specialist supplier. Prior to placing an order, it is a good idea to phone around several suppliers for options and prices. Make sure the quote includes delivery costs.

### Bricks and paving slabs

Bricks and concrete slabs are particularly useful for the projects. We use clay building bricks for edging sumps, and reconstituted concrete slabs for areas of paving. Many reconstituted slabs look so convincing that they cannot be distinguished from the real thing. They are available in all sorts of shapes, sizes, colours and textures, such as tessellating shapes that look like red quarry tiles, sandstone paving slabs, stone on edge, brick slabs and limestone and sandstone flagstones. You can even buy slabs that look as if they have been carved with a picture – these include horse portraits, cottages, Wild West scenes and historical figures such as Horatio Nelson, Buffalo Bill and Sitting Bull.

### Sand, cement and lime

Soft sand, sometimes called builder's sand, is used for making smooth-textured mortar, while sharp sand is used for making concrete and coarse mortars. Sold by the bag or lorry-load, the colour and texture of the sand usually relates to the local stone. If you are looking for good colour and low cost, it would be best to order your sand in bulk from a local pit.

Cement powder – sold in 25 kg and 50 kg bags, and described generically as "Portland cement" – is one of the chief ingredients of mortar and concrete. Though it is undoubtedly true to say that you can save money by ordering large numbers of 50 kg bags, this is the one instance where it is much better to buy only a few small bags for the job in hand. Not only are 50 kg bags difficult to handle, but they are also flimsy and liable to tear, the cement powder is susceptible to damp and loose powder is highly corrosive and very bad for skin, eyes and lungs.

Lime is used together with cement and sand to make mortar. Although a "cement mortar" can be made without lime (which is undoubtedly harder and stronger than lime and cement mortar), it is also so hard that it stains the stone and pulls it apart. As with cement powder, it is best to order lime in small quantities and to be sure to store it in a dry place. Lime is highly corrosive, to the extent that you should wear goggles and a dust-mask when mixing, and gloves for general handling. If cement or lime powder blows in your face when you are mixing, swiftly wash your face and then reposition yourself so that you are working out of the wind. Keep lime away from children and pets.

## WOOD MATERIALS

*Log roll*

*Rough-sawn pine section*

*Railway sleeper*

### Railway sleepers

Several projects use railway sleepers. Second-hand sleepers can be obtained in various lengths and grades at a whole range of prices, from all manner of sources. However, experience has shown us that it is vital to go to the supplier yourself and carefully select individual sleepers, and pay for them as seen. The alternative is to buy them over the phone, and risk receiving a delivery of poor-quality sleepers. You need to specify that the sleepers are "best quality", meaning straight and sound along their length, with no warping or splits, or rusty iron clamps. A good way of checking them is to tap them along their length with a mallet. If they sound

like a drum they are hollow and rotten, and if they ring they are sound. Be wary about cutting sleepers with a power saw, just in case the teeth hit a hidden piece of iron and the saw kicks back. However, if you do want to risk it, be sure to wear gloves and goggles, and follow the manufacturer's safety guidelines.

### Log rolls and rough-sawn pine

Log rolls (split round sections mounted on wire) and general rough-sawn sections are best sourced from your local forestry or garden centre. Make sure that the wood is crisp and dry, and avoid anything that looks mouldy or has loose knots or splits.

# Ponds

A pond breathes life into a garden. An informal natural pond in a secluded corner, or

a formal raised pond in a high-profile position by the patio, gives a garden

atmosphere, sound and movement. It adds a wildlife dimension too – not only can

you stock it with fish, but it will also attract dragonflies, frogs and birds.

> **CAUTION**
>
> Where there are small children, there is no such thing as a safe pond. If you are worried about maintaining adequate supervision, wait until the children are older before you have a pond.

## BUYING TIPS

- For a rigid pond liner, fibreglass is more expensive than plastic, but is stronger and lasts longer.
- There are various grades of flexible liner – everything from inexpensive polythene liners that last for about five years, through to butyl liners that are guaranteed for over 25 years (see page 17). All grades last longer if they are bedded on a layer of sand, fibreglass loft insulation or special fabric.
- To calculate the size of the required liner, add three times the depth of the pond to both the finished length and width.
- Peg out the measurements of the pond in the garden several weeks prior to buying materials. This will help you discover the implications of the size and the siting.

## TYPES OF POND

Basically, there are two types of pond – a formal pond with a hard landscaped edge (brick, stone or tile), and an informal pond designed to blend in with nature. Both types can be built using either a preformed rigid liner, or a flexible plastic liner. Where the formal pond unit sits above ground level, it is generally easier to use a long-lasting preformed rigid liner of fibreglass or plastic.

A pond is going to be there for a long time, so take into account all the constructional, aesthetic and horticultural considerations. For example, are you strong enough to handle the task? Can you afford the materials and equipment? Is your proposed site big enough and correctly orientated? Whatever the type of pond, choose a site that gets at least six hours of sunlight a day, is well away from trees, and has plenty of room for planting.

## HOW TO DESIGN AND MAKE A FORMAL POND

### Design notes

This formal pond uses a rigid fibreglass pool unit set at ground level, and the edge of the unit is covered with concrete slabs. We levelled up the site prior to excavation in order to avoid the problems associated with having one of the edges of the pool unit exposed. When you are buying the unit, look for one that has a generous lip, and check that the entire length of the lip is free from thin areas and cracks, and is generally in a good, sound condition. If the lip is in any way faulty, reject the unit.

### Making a formal pond

**1** Place the unit upside-down on the site and mark the limits with wooden pegs banged into the ground. Measure the depth of the unit and excavate the whole area to that depth, plus 50 mm. Remove the spoil from the site. (Excavated earth may come in handy for another project, such as a cascade or rockery.)

**2** Level the base of the hole with a 50 mm layer of soft sand. Sit the unit in the hole and use a batten and spirit level to check the level across the rim. Gradually backfill between the unit and the earth with soft sand, and compact it with a batten.

**3** Dig a trench around the rim of the pool (300 mm deep and the width of the edging slabs). Fill it with well-compacted hardcore. Space the slabs and bed them on a generous layer of mortar.

*Water*    *Water*    *Concrete slab edging*

*Hardcore*

*Fibreglass pool*

*Sand*

*Hardcore*

*Concrete slab edging*    *Mortar*    *Sand*    *Edge of pool*

ABOVE Plan and cross-section of a straightforward rectangular formal pond made with a preformed fibreglass pool unit, and edged with reconstituted concrete slabs bedded on mortar.

# INFORMAL PONDS

Deep-water plants

Floating plants

Shallow-water marginal plants

Bog garden

Rockery

Large bushes

Moisture-loving plants

Thick liner

Oxygenating plants

Sand

Shelf for marginal plants

ABOVE An informal pond concept that works by imitating nature – a rockery or beach blends into a bog garden, which becomes a pond – so the water looks as if it belongs in the garden.

## Design notes

This pond is made with a flexible liner, allowing for maximum informality. The edges of the pond may incorporate features such as a rockery, bog garden or beach. When you are planning out the pond, allow plenty of space for grading the planting to create a seamless transition between the edge of the water and the far reaches of the surrounding slope. View the pond and its surrounds as a series of terraces, with each step providing a different planting opportunity. So, from the depths of the pond to the heights of the terrace, you might have deep-water plants, shallow-water marginals, plants that enjoy boggy earth, and so on up the slope, ending with plants that are not generally associated with ponds. Site the bog garden in a lined gully around one edge. The best way of planting a pond is to set a few plants in place – the deep-water plants, the marginals and possibly the bog plants – and then slowly add to the planting over one or more seasons. By working gradually, you can achieve a better balance of planting effects. For more details, refer to the Natural Pond project on page 118.

## CONTAINER PONDS

Some gardens are so small that there is not enough space to build a pond, but it is nevertheless possible to create a fully functioning miniature pond. Plastic waterbutts, sunken barrels, tanks, cisterns, troughs or concrete tubs all make water gardens for unlikely and unpromising places such as conservatories, balconies, verandahs and rooftop terraces. The walls of the container need to be thick enough to ensure a constant water temperature. Avoid antique lead cisterns if you have pets that might drink the water.

It is possible to create a water feature that appears to be much larger than it really is, by clever positioning of additional containers. The trick is to plant up the water container with a few choice water plants, and surround it with a good number of containers holding bog plants. Pack other containers, hosting a variety of plants, around these. In this way, it is possible to achieve a planting that seems to range from deep-water plants through to marginals and those that grow on dry banks.

## FISH, FROGS, NEWTS AND OTHER FAUNA

Ponds are much more than a delightful addition to a garden. They also provide a wonderful opportunity to attract water-loving wildlife, which you can enjoy watching. As soon as you have created an area of water – sometimes within hours of finishing the planting around the pond – you will begin to see incredibly beautiful creatures, such as dragonflies and damselflies. Once insects are hovering over the water, they will swiftly be followed by frogs, toads, newts, and all manner of birds and animals.

Many pond lovers are very happy with the wildlife that appears of its own accord, but for others, the main attraction of a pond is that you can have fish in it. The best time for introducing fish is in late spring or early summer, when the water is a suitable temperature. If you decide to stock your pond with fish, you must be prepared to protect the fish from predators such as herons and cats. Hold back from introducing the fish until the pond and its plants have had a chance to get established.

# Pumps and filters

Pumps are used in conjunction with filters to circulate water. They are powered by electricity, so safety considerations are very important. The pump, by means of an impeller, draws water in one end and pushes it out through the other (at which point it is attached to a water feature such as a cascade or fountain).

## HOW TO CHOOSE THE RIGHT PUMP FOR THE JOB

While there are two main types of pump – low-voltage submersible, and high-voltage surface-mounted – this book only uses the former. We chose these because modern, low-voltage submersible pumps are so safe that they can (via an electricity circuit breaker) be plugged directly into an existing socket. You do not have to build a special shed to hold the pump, as it is just placed in the pond. The circuit breaker eliminates the danger of electrocution. If the cable were damaged, the water could be electrified, but a circuit breaker cuts off the power instantly.

The easiest way to calculate the size of pump required is to simply measure the height from the surface of the water to the top of the fountainhead or cascade, and then to purchase a pump with that capacity. Basically, there are four sizes of submersible pump available: a miniature pump designed for mini water features on the patio, a small pump intended for little fountains, a medium-size pump suitable for an average fountain, and a large pump that is big enough to create a cascade. If in doubt about what to buy, describe the project to the supplier and ask for advice, and then get the biggest pump that you can afford – it is then at least possible to cut back on the water flow if necessary.

### BUYING A PUMP

*Questions to answer before you visit the water garden specialist:*
- What is the vertical distance from the surface of the water to the fountainhead nozzle, or the top of the cascade? (This is known as the head height.)
- What is the distance from the pump to the electricity socket?
- How high above the surface of the fountainhead nozzle do you want the water to reach?
- (For a cascade.) What is the horizontal distance between the pump position and the top of the cascade?
- Do you envisage running two or more projects off the same pump in the future? If so, you will need a dual-outlet pump.
- Do you need a separate filtration unit? Most submersible pumps have built-in filters which cope with small volumes of water (a pond that is less than 2 m in diameter for example), but for larger ponds it is better to connect the pump to a filtration unit. A filtration unit at the side of the pond (not in the water) is easier to clean than a submersible pump.

## HOW TO SET UP YOUR PUMP

The position of the pump depends on whether it is going to feed a feature direct, or whether there is a surface filter. The general rule is that if you want it to feed direct, the distance between the pump and the outlet should be as short as possible. If you are fitting a surface filter, the pump must be set up as far away as is practicable from the point at which the water is being returned to the pond.

1 Decide on the position of the pump in the pond, mark out a route for the cables and pipes, and dig a trench leading to the pond. Cover the power cables with a protective sheath, such as

flexible armoured plastic pipe, and set the pipes and cables in the trench.

2 Position the pump in the water (on a slab or a few bricks to keep it away from the sludge), fit the outlet delivery pipes, put the electricity circuit breaker in place, and switch on the power.

3 When you are satisfied with the flow, fill the trench, and make sure that all the pipes and cables are hidden from view.

Buried delivery pipe

Surface filter

Circuit breaker

Buried (protected) power cable

Submerged pump

LEFT An ideal pump and filter arrangement for pond features (such as a cascade) that accumulate dirt and debris in the water.

## LARGE PUMPS

**Fountainhead**
Some are adjustable,
like the nozzle on a
garden hosepipe

**Screw**
Make sure
that the
connector fits
your chosen
fountainhead

**Push-fit connector**
Check that
this is
suitable for
your set-up

**Screw-fit connector**
Ensures
secure joints

**T-junction**
Facility for a tap and
a second outlet pipe

**Telescopic outlet pipe**
Extends telescopically
to suit different depths

**Integral adjuster**
Rotates to
restrict flow

**Pump and filter housing**

**Power selector**

**Fixing plates**

## MEDIUM PUMPS

**Alternative spray nozzle**
Designed to fit into the
nozzle adapter

**Fountainhead spray nozzle**
Produces a fine spray

**Nozzle adapter**

**Alternative fountainhead**
The spray
pattern is
shaped by the
size and position
of the holes

**Telescopic outlet pipe**

**Filter block**

**Filter casing**

**Lifting handle**

**Fixing point**

A medium-size submersible pump with its own integral filter is a good option for a dedicated pump to run a single feature, for example a fountain or water course. (Small pumps are the same, with a smaller capacity.) Such pumps are usually supplied with a range of fountainheads and an extension tube that can be adjusted according to water depth. Choose a pump that is designed to be stripped down and cleaned, and one that comes with a spare filter. (Some pumps are sold as sealed units.) When the water flow slows down because of a build-up of sludge on the filter, you simply remove the filter sponge from the casing and wash it.

Large submersible pumps are designed to deliver a good flow of water to one or more outlets, for example a fountain and a water filter. They are able to handle a small amount of mud and sludge without the impeller clogging and grinding to a halt. Such pumps are usually fitted with an integral adjuster that allows you to govern the rate of flow, and a tap that allows you to cut off one of the two outlets. The pump should be cleaned out at least once a week during the running season. Although it needs regular attention to stay in good working order, it is inexpensive and will last for a long time. Assume that the manufacturer's rating of a pump's performance relates to perfect conditions (or is over-optimistic) and buy a pump that appears to exceed your requirements.

## MINIATURE PUMPS

**Outlet pipe**
A length of pipe
or a connector
fits on to this

**Sucker foot**
Fixes the pump to
base of container

Miniature pumps are designed specifically for container water features, when you want a pump that is small enough to tuck away under gravel or rocks. They are only capable of powering a small dribble fountain, but are maintenance-free and run silently. It is still essential to plug in this type of pump via an electricity circuit breaker. For safety, if you have children, always buy a pump that the manufacturer describes as "child friendly".

# Fountains

Fountains are magical! The moment you install a pump complete with a statuette

and spray, or a pump with a fountainhead that just breaks the surface of the water

in a pond, you create a wonderfully dynamic effect. Fountains are also supremely

practical, in that the movement enriches the water with oxygen.

> **CAUTION**
>
> Even though most manufacturers declare that low-voltage fountain pumps are totally safe, it is still a good idea to fit an electricity circuit breaker and to protect the power cable.

## DECORATIVE AND PRACTICAL USES OF FOUNTAINS

### Ornamental fountains

A standard fountain pump comes complete with an extension pipe and a selection of fountainhead spray nozzles. You can either mount the unit directly in the water and simply adjust your chosen nozzle for best effect, or you can fit the pump under a decorative statuette. Connecting the unit directly produces the largest possible spray height above the surface of the water. When the unit is mounted under a statuette, you have to take the height of the statuette into account when you are working out the total height of the spray that can be achieved. For example, if the pump gives a spray height of 500 mm above the water, and it is run through a statuette that is 250 mm high, then it follows that the spray will only push 250 mm above the top of the statuette. So if you want a statuette fountain with a dramatic spray, it is best to buy the statuette first, and then choose a pump size that relates to the height of the statuette. Visit garden centres and specialist suppliers to see the various fountains and sprays in action. Take notes, keep the brochures and generally research the whole project before you make a purchase.

### Oxygenating fountains

Oxygen is necessary for the fish and wildlife of a pond. If a fountain's primary function is to oxygenate the water, select the largest pump that you can afford and fit it directly to the fountainhead nozzle, setting the nozzle to produce the most complex spray formation. The greater the turbulence in the water, the greater the amount of oxygen produced: a geyser fountain with a dense, foaming plume will generate more oxygen than a bell jet.

## TYPES OF FOUNTAIN PATTERN

ABOVE Geyser fountain: exciting and slightly erratic, and a good choice for an open, breezy site.

ABOVE Bell jet fountain: gives a structured effect that is good for a small, formal pond.

ABOVE Single spray nozzle: a good choice when you want to create a bold, dynamic effect.

ABOVE Fountain jet: a simple no-fuss fountain that is low-cost and looks good in any pond.

### Flow control

The vertical distance between the surface of the water and the top of the fountainhead nozzle is called the head height of the water. Maximum head height can be achieved by a pump if the fountain is fitted with a narrow-gauge delivery pipe and the water is clean, but if the delivery pipe is wide and badly fitted, and there is lots of mud in the water, the head height will be much reduced. Check that all the fittings are tight and the pump is working efficiently, push your chosen nozzle on the extension pipe, check that the flow adjuster is set for maximum pressure and minimum flow, and then switch on the power. Finally, fine-tune your chosen nozzle according to the manufacturer's instructions.

When experimenting with the pump, make sure that your hands and the water are clean, because grit will affect the flow of the water. Check that the nozzle size relates to the size of the chosen pump, or you may be disappointed by the effect.

## SETTING UP A SIMPLE FOUNTAIN

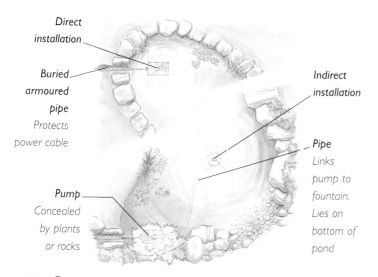

Direct installation

Buried armoured pipe
*Protects power cable*

Indirect installation

Pipe
*Links pump to fountain. Lies on bottom of pond*

Pump
*Concealed by plants or rocks*

ABOVE Direct installation (top): the pump is underneath the fountain. Indirect installation (bottom): the pump is by the side of the pond.

### Direct installation

Fountains can be installed directly or indirectly. When a fountain is directly installed, the fountainhead nozzle leads straight off a submersible pump via a vertical extension tube, with the pump sitting on a plinth of bricks or concrete slabs at the bottom of the pond. The very simplest type of set-up has the pump positioned as near as possible to the edge of the pond (for easy access), and no attempt is made to conceal it. This arrangement looks a bit basic, but its advantage is that the pump works at maximum efficiency.

### Indirect installation

With an indirect or remote installation, the submersible pump feeds the fountainhead via a flexible tube that runs horizontally across the bottom of the pond. In this arrangement, the pump can be concealed just about anywhere in the pond, and the fountainhead is remote from the pump. The pump is easily accessible, but the reduced efficiency cuts down the height of the spray.

## ORNAMENTAL FOUNTAINS

### Design notes

It is best to choose an ornamental statuette first, and then select a pump that is powerful enough to force water through the ornament and to at least the same height again. A direct installation, as described below (and on page 48), is the easiest and cheapest method of setting it up, and therefore ideal for the beginner.

### Procedure for setting up an ornamental fountain

**1** Position the submersible pump on a plinth (a concrete slab, or a few bricks) in the pond and arrange the electric cable so that it is hidden from view. Place the housing over the pump and switch on the power to check the water flow.

**2** Fit a flexible extension hose to the pump and secure it with a hose clip. Join the other end of the extension hose to the pipe on the underside of the ornamental statuette, and fix with a hose clip. Put the statuette in position on the housing.

**3** Fit the fountainhead nozzle on the statuette. Having put the electricity circuit breaker in place and made sure that it is operational, switch on the power and test the flow and the shape of the spray. Adjust the rate of flow and the nozzle accordingly.

RIGHT A cross-section through a typical ornamental statuette fountain. The statuette is an immediate eye-catcher and perfect for enhancing a small garden pond.

Spray
*Height controlled by the pump*

Fountainhead nozzle
*Can be adjusted*

Ornamental statuette
*Pipe already cast through the centre*

Water

Flexible extension hose

Hose clip

Submersible pump

Brick plinth

Thick pond liner

Housing to support statue

Hidden power cable

Sand

Soil

# Cascades, canals and bogs

A basic pond is not just an attractive feature in its own right. It can also be used as a reservoir for feeding other garden water features such as a cascade waterfall (which could also extend into a water rockery), a formal patio or courtyard canal, or a bog garden. The moment the pond is in place, you can start planning.

## DESIGNING AND MAKING CASCADES

**Outlet pipe**
Supplies water to the top header pool. The end of the pipe is raised above the level of the water

**Stones**
For decoration

**Precast unit**
The lip needs to overlap the unit below

**Final precast unit**
Hangs over the edge of the pond

**Compacted earth**
Earth packed under the units to obtain the desired angle

**Water outlet pipe**
Buried and hidden from view, running from the pump to the header pool

**Thick pond liner**
Bedded on sand to create the main reservoir pool for the pump

**Pond**
The pond or reservoir pool needs to be big enough to contain a concealed pump

**Pump**
A large and powerful pump is required

LEFT A cross-section through a cascade made from precast shop-bought units, terraced earth and stones. This is a quick way to make a cascade; an alternative method is to use thick pond liner instead of the precast units.

## Design notes

In essence, a cascade is a series of stepped pools, with a header pool at the top end and a reservoir at the bottom. The first problem you have to sort out is how to achieve the actual slope of the cascade. If your garden is on a slope and you want to build a big cascade, you do not need to do any landscaping; otherwise you have to import earth to make a little hillock.

If you are limited to a patio or roof garden, you can still have a cascade, although on a smaller scale – think in terms of a pot or container cascade. For a swift, easy answer, there are lots of kits for container cascades on the market, which contain the pump, container, and everything you need.

## Building a cascade from precast units

Having excavated and built your pond, heaping the spoil to the side, take the first precast unit and bed it at the bottom of the mound of earth, so that it is hanging just over the edge of the

pond. Fill the unit with water and adjust it (by packing earth underneath it) so that the water begins to run over the lip and into the pond. Take the second unit and lap it over the first, compacting the earth beneath it beforehand. Fill it with water and adjust its level (again by packing earth underneath it) so that the water overflows into the first unit and back into the pond. Continue lapping one unit over another until you get to the top of the slope. When you are pleased with the way the water flows, bolt or clip the units together.

Sit the pump in the pond, and run the water outlet pipe from the pond back up the slope of earth to the topmost unit. Bury the cables and pipes, landscape the whole mound much as you would a rockery, and plant out the area. Watch the performance of the cascade over several days to make sure it is working correctly. Check the water level when it is all switched off. If it is too low, there may be leaks in the system (tighten the hose clips), or you may need to adjust the way the plastic units lap over each other.

## DESIGNING AND MAKING CANALS

*Pump*

*Pond*

*Canal liner*
*Plastic sheet*

*Hardcore*
*100 mm deep*

*Header pool*
*Overflowing into canal*

*Delivery pipe*
*The end of the pipe is above the water level to prevent backward flow*

*Pond liner*

*Soil*

*Stones and pavers*
*Arranged in the canal to create dynamic water movement*

*Concrete*

*Delivery pipe outlet*
*Positioned to be clear of the water*

*Header pool*
*Set at a higher level than the canal*

*Pond reservoir*

*Buried water delivery pipe*

ABOVE AND RIGHT **A cross-section (above) and overview (right) of a canal design giving the illusion of a never-ending supply of water.**

### Design notes

To construct a canal, water is pumped into a header pool that overflows into a straight channel, then into a pond. This is similar to a cascade – water is pumped from a pond to a header pool, where it then flows back to the pond. The good thing about a canal is that it can be built with little or no gradient, so if you are limited by a level site, but want some moving water, a canal is a good compromise. Dramatic designs may channel water across a paved area or even a lawn – the proviso being that the water must be contained and not drain away. The size of the pump governs the amount of water overflowing from the header pool.

### Building a canal

Dig a shallow trench for the canal. One end should run into the pond. Check with a spirit level that it is just about level, or at least only sloping slightly (towards the pond). Fill the trench with 100 mm hardcore, and top with concrete. Line with plastic sheet, and edge the canal with concrete slabs and bricks. Set the pump in the pond and bury the delivery pipe alongside the trench, with the outlet overhanging the top end of the canal. Cover the outlet pipe with a slab. Scatter a few flat slates, broken pavers and small stones along the canal bed to create interesting water movement. Finally, fit an electricity circuit breaker.

## MAKING A BOG GARDEN

Bog gardens – made by planting up shallow boggy areas around the margins of a pond – can be used not only to enhance a pond and make it appear much larger than it is, but also to provide an environment for water-loving plants and wildlife.

Dig a gully (about 500 mm deep) around the edge of the pond. Line it with inexpensive plastic sheet, piercing a few drainage holes, and cover with a shallow layer of shingle. Mix the excavated soil with lots of well-rotted organic matter, and put it back in the gully. When it rains, the flow-off from the pond will help keep the gully damp, making an area that is ideally suited to water-loving plants. Once the plants are in place, insects, birds, and amphibious creatures such as frogs, toads and newts will make an appearance.

RIGHT **A cross-section through the edge of a pond and bog area. Note that the pond liner encompasses the bog area, at which point it is pierced to allow a degree of drainage.**

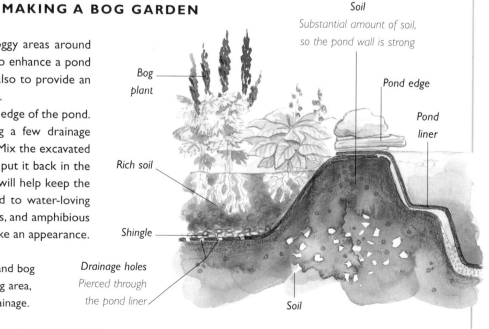

*Soil*
*Substantial amount of soil, so the pond wall is strong*

*Bog plant*

*Pond edge*

*Pond liner*

*Rich soil*

*Shingle*

*Drainage holes*
*Pierced through the pond liner*

*Soil*

# Plants for water features

One of the chief pleasures of a water feature is that it provides an exciting environment for planting. One moment you have a lawn and a patio, and borders filled with the usual annuals and perennials, and the next you have the opportunity to extend your planting range with a vast assortment of water- and moisture-loving plants.

## THE ROLE OF PLANTS FOR WATER FEATURES

### Keeping the water healthy

While a pump, filter and fountain can be used to keep water clear, the whole task can be achieved more efficiently by choosing the right plants. You need submerged oxygenating plants to release oxygen into the water – good for fish and wildlife – and floating broad-leaf plants to use up some of the excess nutriments. The trick is getting the balance right. If there are too few plants, the water soon gets slimy and green, too many broad-leaf plants make the water get clogged up with debris, too few broad-leaf plants allow the sunlight to penetrate the water and overstimulate the growth of green algae. Be prepared to remove plants that start to dominate, or plants that fail.

### Food for all

Water plants maintain the oxygen levels of the water in the pond, but they are also needed to maintain the overall cycle of life in the pond. The chain of events in the pond cycle is as follows: the plants produce oxygen and use up carbon dioxide; insects and animals eat the plants, use oxygen and produce carbon dioxide, and eat each other; the waste from animals and insects produces mineral salts, which plants need for healthy growth; plant debris is eaten by water snails and other creatures.

If you notice that one of the elements is beginning to dominate – too much algae, too many snails or whatever – it means that there is an imbalance in the pond that needs to be corrected.

## DEEP-WATER PLANTS

### Plant choice

Some deep-water plants live with their roots in deep water and have foliage growing both below and on the surface of the water, others are floating plants that drift around the pond, and certain plants grow totally below the surface of the water. Many people are keen to try water-lilies because they are so attractive, but the variety has to be carefully chosen to suit the size of the pond and the depth of water. In ideal conditions, most deep-water plants are fast-growing, so much so that they need to be regularly thinned.

### Planting

While plants such as water-lilies need to be planted with their roots in a container on the floor of the pond, the floaters and the underwater oxygenators can simply be tossed into the water. The best way of planting bare-rooted plants such as water-lilies, is to remove all damaged foliage, cut away straggly roots, wash off all traces of algae, and insert the root system in a plastic planting basket filled with aquatic compost. The basket is positioned (on a stack of bricks if necessary) at the bottom of the pond.

RIGHT A detail showing plants in basket containers sited on the bottom of the deepest part of the pond. The leaves of the water-lily check the growth of algae, and the submerged plant pumps oxygen into the water.

*Water-lilies*
*The leaves float on the surface, but the roots need to be in the deep area of the pond*

*Oxygenating plants*
*Placed at the bottom of the pond*

# MARGINAL PLANTS

## Plant choice

Marginal plants thrive in the shallow water around the edge or margins of a pond. Characteristically, marginal plants have strong vertical top growth, and relatively shallow root systems. While most marginals are at their best when their roots are actually in the water, many varieties are just as happy in the soil at the water's edge. Bog plants are suitable for this area. Some marginals produce strong, spiky roots that are capable of piercing plastic pond liners, so choose the varieties with care.

## Planting

A planting scheme has to be planned to take into account both the idiosyncracies of the plants and their visual effect. Preferred water depths range from 300 mm through to 20 mm, some plants thrive in mud rather than water, and foliage height varies enormously. It's a good idea to have the plants with the lowest foliage on the shelved edge of the pond, and more vigorous plants in the mud at the water's edge. Experiment with various placings before you actually finalize their position on bank, shelf or underwater.

*Shelf*
*At the side of the pond*

*Planting depth*

*Shallow root system*
*In saturated soil, at the edge of the pond*

ABOVE A marginal plant (left) sited on a shelf in the pond which raises it to an appropriate planting depth. On the right, a bog plant that likes the very damp or wet soil alongside the pond.

# MOISTURE-LOVING PLANTS

*Moisture-loving plant*
*Planted in damp soil*

*Large plants*
*A stone is placed between the plant and the edge of the pond to prevent the roots from damaging the liner*

ABOVE Many of your garden plants will benefit by being moved closer to the water's edge. Beware of plants that have strong root systems.

## Plant choice

Moisture-loving plants are best defined as plants that thrive in a moist environment – damp earth and a high humidity. They are perfect for linking features such as ponds and cascades to the beds in the rest of the garden. Be careful not to confuse bog plants with moisture-loving plants. The important difference between them is that while some moisture-loving plants will tolerate boggy soil conditions, mostly they prefer damp soil that is well drained and never waterlogged. When you are choosing plants, it is much better to select varieties that will thrive in damp soil, rather than plants that merely tolerate damp conditions. For best performance, you want plants that are totally happy, rather than plants that are making the best of a bad job!

## Planting

Prepare the bed with lots of well-rotted organic material, and dig in clay granules if the soil is very sandy. Make sure that the ground remains damp but is not subject to waterlogging. Before buying a plant, find out whether its root depth and foliage height are suitable for the site. Try to grade the foliage height of the planting scheme as it moves away from the pond, so that your eye is gradually led up from the water's edge, and the foliage reaches maximum height with the moisture-loving plants. If you have doubts about the suitability of a plant, buy a small example and plant it to see whether it thrives in the given conditions. It is a good idea to visit all your local garden centres and water garden specialists, where hopefully you will see good examples of planting, and pick up some ideas before making your purchases.

# Maintenance

For many people, part of the pleasure of having a pond complete with a pump, fountain, lots of plants, a fish or two, and perhaps a colony of frogs, is the fun involved in keeping the whole set-up in good condition. If you enjoyed playing with water and mud as a child, you'll be in your element.

## POND MAINTENANCE

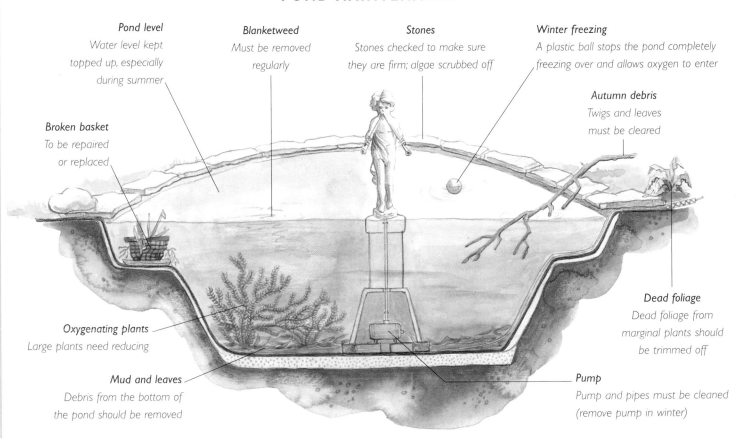

**Pond level**
Water level kept topped up, especially during summer

**Blanketweed**
Must be removed regularly

**Stones**
Stones checked to make sure they are firm; algae scrubbed off

**Winter freezing**
A plastic ball stops the pond completely freezing over and allows oxygen to enter

**Autumn debris**
Twigs and leaves must be cleared

**Broken basket**
To be repaired or replaced

**Oxygenating plants**
Large plants need reducing

**Mud and leaves**
Debris from the bottom of the pond should be removed

**Dead foliage**
Dead foliage from marginal plants should be trimmed off

**Pump**
Pump and pipes must be cleaned (remove pump in winter)

## Cleaning the pond

Clean out the pond in the spring, when the leaf fall of the previous autumn is over and before all the pond plants start into new growth. Use a net on a stick to scoop out dead leaves and twigs. Remove all plants growing in baskets and pull off damaged foliage. Wash the plants and do your best to scrub off all traces of algae. If necessary, repair broken plant baskets with wire and fill them up with fresh soil and grit.

During the cleaning process, be very careful that you do not injure the fish, snails, frogs or anything else living in the mud. Finally, replace all the plants and top up the pond with water. If the pond is so wide that you cannot reach the middle with your net, ask a friend to help. Make a large scoop or drag net (a rectilinear frame of garden wire, with an old net curtain stretched across), and rig it with two long, strong ropes. Working on opposite sides of the pond, take turns pulling the net across.

### CAUTION

During pond maintenance, make sure that you do not damage the liner. Avoid using sharp items such as sticks and garden rakes. Choose rakes with soft plastic prongs and nets with plastic hoops.

## Hot and cold weather maintenance

Extreme weather conditions necessitate taking measures to protect the plants and wildlife from damage. In order to maintain the equilibrium of the pond in hot weather, you must check the pond every day and make sure it is topped up with water. If you see the fish gulping for air or notice that the algae is multiplying, then the chances are the pond needs more water and additional oxygenating plants.

In freezing weather, it is a good idea to float a large plastic ball on the water. The movement of the ball will prevent a small area from freezing over, and this clear water not only acts as a vent for toxic gases, but also helps reduce the pressure of the ice on the sides of the pond. Never try to break the ice on a pond with a spike or a hammer. The vibration may have an adverse effect on the fish, you might slip and fall in the pond, and you could drop the tool and damage the liner.

## Removing algae

When a build-up of algae or blanketweed (*Spirogyra*) begins to choke the pond, take a couple of bamboo canes and use them to carefully tease the blanketweed away from the various plants. With a cane in each hand, use one cane to support the plant, while poking the other cane into the blanketweed. Roll the weed cane until it takes on a mass of green, and then pull the weed out of the water and wipe it off into a bucket. Continue teasing the weed away from the plants and rolling it on to the cane until the whole mess has been removed from the pond.

## Routine plant care

Caring for pond plants is an ongoing procedure that runs right across the year, but spring and summer are the busiest. Spring is the time to clean out the pond, trim decaying leaves from the plants, and remove debris with a scoop net. Do not be tempted to use a lawn rake or fork to remove debris, because if you lose concentration and the tool slips into the pond, you will be left with a punctured pond liner that needs repairing.

You might also need to thin out some of the more rampant oxygenators and divide up clumps of floating plants. Scoop out the plants, divide them up on the bank, and then return small, healthy sections to the pond. Spring is also a good time for reassessing the combination of plants in the pond. You may wish to increase your stock and introduce new plants to the pond. Or if you have too many of a particular plant, now is the time for a cull.

In summer you will need to be constantly trimming off yellowing and dying leaves and shaping up plants, in order to ensure that the pond stays clear of decaying matter and so that plants are encouraged to produce new flowerheads. When you are removing weed and decaying leaves, don't just throw them on the compost heap, but wash them in a bucket of pond water to remove all the small creatures such as water boatmen and snails, and carefully return these to the pond. When you are cleaning out debris, be careful not to let any seed pods fall to the bottom of the pond, or you'll have a crop of unwanted plants.

If you want to introduce new plants and yet you are also worried about introducing unwanted creatures, leave the new plants in a bucket of water for a few days – in a sort of watery quarantine – and wash them prior to putting them into the pond.

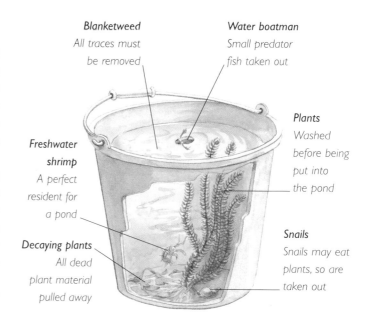

*Blanketweed*
*All traces must be removed*

*Water boatman*
*Small predator fish taken out*

*Freshwater shrimp*
*A perfect resident for a pond*

*Decaying plants*
*All dead plant material pulled away*

*Plants*
*Washed before being put into the pond*

*Snails*
*Snails may eat plants, so are taken out*

ABOVE When you buy new plants, use a quarantine bucket (kept away from your pond) which allows you to select precisely what you do and don't want to introduce into your pond.

*Outlet pipe*
*Clean inside the pipe with a small brush*

*Impeller*
*Rotate (by hand) under running water to clear debris*

*Nozzle*
*Clear blockages with a pin*

*Foam filter*
*Take off casing, remove and rinse out*

ABOVE Clean your pump regularly. If dirt and weed builds up in the filter, the pump will lose power and then grind to a halt. Turn off the power as soon as you notice a pump has stopped working.

## PUMP MAINTENANCE

The efficiency of a pump will soon be affected if the water is muddy. At least once a week in high summer, switch off the power, remove the pump from the water, and service it as follows. Ease the casing apart, take out the foam filter and wash it in warm water and non-scented liquid soap. Squeeze the foam repeatedly to break down the compacted mud that collects at its centre. Disassemble the pump and the various fountain pipes and connections, and wash them in warm water and liquid soap. Use a small brush to clean inside the pipes. Turn the impeller round under running water to remove all traces of grit, so that it spins freely with the minimum of friction. Finally, wash the whole pump under running water to remove the soap, and put it back in the water.

On no account try to speed up the cleaning procedure by using a spirit-based solvent, and do not attempt to ease the bearings by using oil. Both these substances will pollute the water in the pond and damage fish and plants. Make sure, when you are testing the pump prior to putting it back into the water feature, that you connect it up via an electricity circuit breaker.

# Part 2: **Projects**

# Container bog garden

**If you would like to have a water garden, but are short of space, or you simply want to try working on something very basic before going on to greater things, a container bog garden is the answer. The waterlogged soil is perfect for a wide range of bog plants. Garden centres often group plants that enjoy wet, well-drained soil together with those that prefer boggy conditions, so make sure that the plant you choose is happy in waterlogged soil, such as one of the water irises.**

### TIME

One day (two hours to prepare the containers and pot the plant, and the rest of the day for the resin sealant to cure).

### SAFETY

If you are allergic to resin, wear protective gloves and follow the manufacturer's advice closely.

## YOU WILL NEED

**Materials** *for a container bog garden 450 mm in diameter and 300 mm high*
- Ceramic outer container: about 450 mm in diameter and 200 mm deep
- Wine bottle corks (to plug the drainage holes in the outer container)
- Resin sealant (for use inside outer container if it is porous): amount to suit the size of your chosen pot

- Washed shingle (small): 1 bucketful
- Ceramic inner container: about 300 mm in diameter and 250 mm deep with drainage holes
- Broken plant pot crocks
- Soil and organic matter mix suitable for plant
- A bog plant

**Tools**
- Disposable container
- Paintbrush: 30 mm wide

## BOG PLANT BEAUTY

Choose two ceramic containers that complement each other in colour or shape. The large outer pot needs to be low and broad, the inner pot relatively tall and slender, and both pots require a strong rim or lip. Ideally, the outer pot needs to be glazed inside and out (or made from non-porous stoneware), and to have no drainage holes. But such pots are very difficult to find, so at the very least make sure that your chosen pot is glazed on the outside. Any drainage holes will be plugged with corks.

Avoid traditional non-glazed earthenware flowerpots, because they are thin-bodied, fragile and porous. To test the porosity of a pot, dab it with a wet finger and see what happens to the moisture. If it sits on the surface like a bead, the pot is non-porous, whereas if it is soaked up, the pot is porous. Before you make your final choice, sit the pots one within the other, make allowances for the depth of the gravel, and see how they look together.

## CROSS-SECTION OF THE BOG GARDEN

*Bog plant*
Ask your local nursery to recommend a species

*Inner container*
300 mm in diameter and 250 mm deep

*Soil*
To suit your chosen plant

*Water*

*Shingle*

*Outer container*
450 mm in diameter and 200 mm deep

## Step-by-step: Making the container bog garden

*Porosity*
*If the pot is glazed on the inside you can miss out step 2*

**1** Take the outer container, and plug any drainage holes. Dip the corks in the resin sealant and push them into the drainage holes. When you have achieved a tight fit, dribble more sealant around the corks.

*Tight fit*
*Make sure that the cork plugs the hole effectively*

*Cork*
*The corks must be dry when you put them in the holes*

*Sealing*
*For porous containers. Let the sealant dry between coats*

*Compacting*
*Press the shingle down to make a firm bed*

*Coverage*
*Very porous ceramic may need extra coats of sealant*

*Shingle*
*Use nicely coloured, rounded pebbles*

**2** Pour sealant into the disposable container and thin to a wash with water. Use the paintbrush to brush three or more generous coats of sealant over the inside of the bowl (until you consider it is watertight), and leave it to dry.

**3** Spread shingle inside the container, filling the pot to about half its total depth. Be careful not to dislodge the corks.

*Cleaning*
*Wash out the container*
*first if it is dirty*

**4** Take the inner container and place a layer of broken crocks over the drainage holes. Fill it with soil mix, then pot up your chosen bog plant.

*Blocking the holes*
*Wash broken crocks and lay them to cover the drainage holes*

*Handling*
*Be careful not to crack the containers – they can be very fragile*

**5** Put the inner container in position, and then very carefully fill the outer bowl with water to within 50 mm of the rim. Check for leakage, wait awhile for the soil to become waterlogged, and then adjust the level of the water.

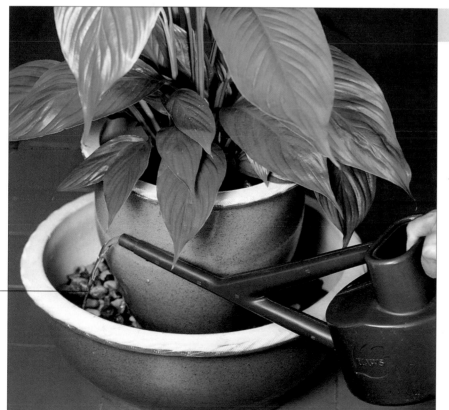

*Water level*
*Inspect the water level every day and keep it topped up to within 50 mm of the rim*

### Helpful hint

Check the water daily and adjust the level to suit the needs of your chosen plant. Get into the routine of filling the watering can and leaving it to stand overnight, so that the water added to the plant is at a constant temperature.

# Wall mask waterspout

An enclosed patio or courtyard is wonderfully enhanced by the addition of a classical

mask waterspout. The mask is set into a wall and water gently trickles from it into a

decorative reservoir pool. The sight and sound of the water sparkling as it falls

soothe the senses beautifully – the whole effect is truly magical!

**TIME**

Two days to prepare the
planter and fix the mask
(allow seven days for the
mortar to cure).

**SPECIAL TIP**

The electrics must be
protected by an electricity
circuit breaker, which will
instantly cut off the
electricity supply if the pump
or cable is damaged.

## YOU WILL NEED

### Materials

- Plastic rainwater pipe:
  250 mm long and 60 mm
  in diameter
- Mortar: 1 part (25 kg)
  cement, 3 parts (75 kg)
  sharp sand
- Mask made of cast lead,
  plastic, ceramic or concrete
- Heavy-duty plastic hosepipe:
  3 m long and 20 mm in
  diameter (the type that will
  go around corners without
  deforming)
- Roofing slate: 1 slate
- Submersible pump with cable
- Flexible armoured plastic
  pipe (long enough to
  protect the full length of
  the pump's electric cable)
- Electricity circuit breaker
- Silicone sealant

- Waterproof sealant: 1 litre
- Screws: 4 x 60 mm long
- Hose clips: 2 x 20 mm clips
- Bracket and clips to fix
  hosepipe: 2 x 20 mm clips

### Tools

- Tape measure and a piece
  of chalk
- Mason's hammer
- Cold chisel
- Wheelbarrow
- Bucket
- Shovel
- Bricklayer's trowel
- Mortar float
- Electric hammer drill with a
  20 mm masonry bit
- Club hammer
- Pointing trowel
- Paintbrush
- Screwdriver

## FALLING WATER

Study the site and decide on the best position for the waterspout,
the type of reservoir you want, and the route for the electricity.
For the reservoir, you can either adapt an existing raised bed as
shown, or use an old sink, stone tub, ceramic bowl or reservoir
kit. Measure the head of water (from the water level in the
reservoir to the mask spout) and purchase a submersible
pump to suit. The pump is set on a brick, with both the electric cable and the hose running through a short length of
plastic rainwater pipe, which protects them from being
crushed by the wall. For extra protection, the cable is passed
through an armoured plastic pipe. Water is pumped from the
reservoir, through the wall, up to the mask, and through the spout.
It then drops on to the slate and dribbles back to the reservoir.

CROSS-SECTION OF THE WALL MASK WATERSPOUT

**Fixings**
Mask is fixed with
plugs and screws

**Wall**
Solid brick
garden wall

**Mask**
Cast lead mask

**Spout**
Hosepipe pushes
on to the spout

**Heavy-duty
hosepipe**
3 m x 20 mm
Fixed to
the wall

**Slate**
Water splashes
over the slate

**Lining**
Container is
rendered

**Reservoir**

**Plastic rainwater
pipe**
250 x 60 mm
Protects the
hosepipe

**Electrics**
Armoured pipe
protects the
electric cable

**Pump**
Medium size

**Brick**
A brick raises the
pump and keeps it clear
from sludge build-up

## Step-by-step: Making the wall mask waterspout

*Cleaning*
*Remove the earth and plants and wash the area clean*

*Spout hole*
*Ensure that you drill at right angles to the wall*

*Render*
*The reservoir needs to be made waterproof*

*Hammer drill*
*Use a hammer drill and a masonry bit*

*Mask*
*Use the mask to establish the position of the spout hole*

**1** Remove the contents of the raised bed. Using the mason's hammer and cold chisel, chop a hole, 70 mm in diameter, through the bottom part of the wall and into the bed. Slide the plastic rainwater pipe in place and render the interior of the bed with mortar, using the bricklayer's trowel and the mortar float.

**2** Holding the mask in place, establish the precise position of the spout hole, and then drill a hole through the thickness of the wall. It must be wide enough for the hosepipe.

*Chisel*
*Use a good-quality cold chisel to chop out the mortar*

**3** Ease one end of the hosepipe through the hole in the wall. Establish the position of the slate in relation to your chosen mask, and use the club hammer and cold chisel to chop out the mortar to make a slot to hold the slate. Adjust the slate so that it will interrupt the water flow. Use the pointing trowel to fix it in place with mortar.

*Gloves*
*You may slip with the hammer, so wear gloves to protect your hands*

*Covering*
*To avoid filling the reservoir with dust and grit, which will block the pump, cover the top with a plastic bag or something similar*

*Slate*
*Interrupts the falling water so the stream*
*is diffused as it enters the pool*

**4** Set the pump in place in the trough and pass the pump's electric cable through the armoured plastic pipe. Fit an electricity circuit breaker. Pull the other end of the hosepipe through into the reservoir, and push it on to the pump outlet. Stop the rainwater pipe with mortar and cap it off with a squirt of silicone sealant.

*Hosepipe*
*The hosepipe*
*should fit tightly*
*on to the pump*

*Alignment*
*Check that the*
*mask, slate and*
*centre of the*
*reservoir are*
*in line with*
*each other*

**5** Brush a generous coat of waterproof sealant over the interior of the whole reservoir. With the screwdriver, screw the mask in place, push the hosepipe on to the spout and fix with the hose clips. Fit the hosepipe to the back of the wall with brackets and bracket clips. Wait seven days for the mortar and sealant to cure before turning on the waterspout's water supply.

### *Helpful hint*

If the delivery of water is slow or no more than a dribble, check to make sure that the water hose isn't deformed at the point where it enters the wall.

## Inspirations: Wall masks

A classical mask peeping out from behind a curtain of foliage – perhaps the face of an ancient Greek god – is a wonderful, mood-setting feature. It instantly imparts a sense of history to any space. Modern masks can be used to enhance a variety of garden themes. A Japanese mask would complement an austere gravel and stone Japanese garden. Dramatic African or Indian masks would combine well with tropical plants. And masks by artists can be used to inject wit, humour and theatrical effect.

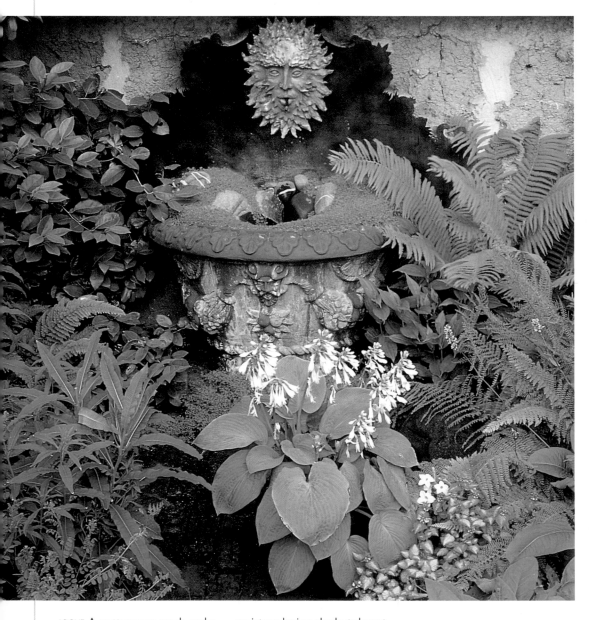

ABOVE **A pottery sun mask, and a terracotta urn adorned with classical imagery, focus attention on this half-hidden niche at the end of a path. Surrounded by** moisture-loving, shade-tolerant plants, this is a beautiful and tranquil corner. The mask spouts a fine stream of water for visual and musical effect.

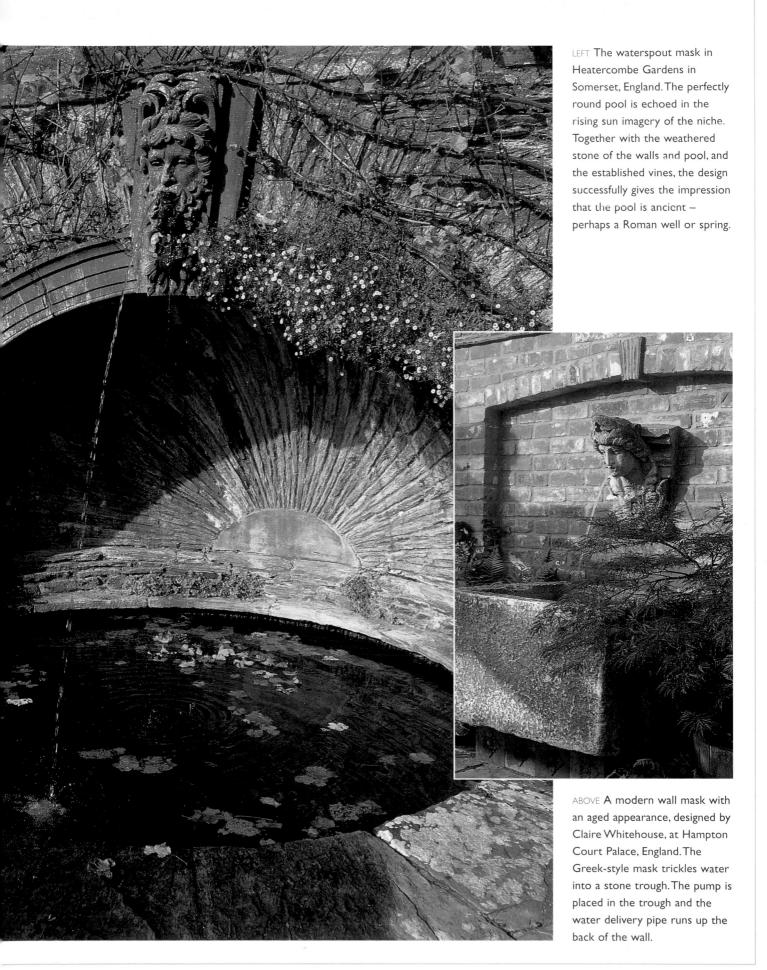

LEFT The waterspout mask in Heatercombe Gardens in Somerset, England. The perfectly round pool is echoed in the rising sun imagery of the niche. Together with the weathered stone of the walls and pool, and the established vines, the design successfully gives the impression that the pool is ancient – perhaps a Roman well or spring.

ABOVE A modern wall mask with an aged appearance, designed by Claire Whitehouse, at Hampton Court Palace, England. The Greek-style mask trickles water into a stone trough. The pump is placed in the trough and the water delivery pipe runs up the back of the wall.

# Mini marble fountain

A fountain gently spouting and overflowing, marbles and pebbles glistening in the water, goldfish shimmering in the sun: this project has all of these. Although the fountain is tiny and the goldfish are made from copper, it is delightful and would be perfect on a patio or as a centrepiece to bring good Feng Shui to a courtyard.

### TIME

One day (three hours to prepare the containers and position the pump, and the rest of the day to complete).

### SAFETY

Some mini pumps are not suitable for outdoor use, so check before you buy.

## PLAN VIEW OF THE MINI MARBLE FOUNTAIN

Fountain container
320 mm in diameter
and 180 mm deep

Fountainhead

Copper fish

Water falls over sides

Shingle

Marble

Wire mesh

Pump

Cable off-cut

Liner

Reservoir container
520 mm in diameter
and 180 mm deep

Tape
Pipe bound with tape
to form a plug

Flowerpot
200 mm in diameter
and 130 mm deep

## DESIGN FOR COPPER FISH

Eye hole
Punched or drilled

Copper
70 mm long,
23 mm wide
and 1 mm
(or less) thick

(PLAN VIEW)

Copper is bent into this shape

## A FOUNTAIN AND A BRIMMING POOL

In essence the project is made up from three ceramic containers – a large, wide pot for the main reservoir, a medium-sized pot for the fountain, and a small flowerpot to contain and conceal the pump and support the fountain pot. The reservoir container can be glazed or unglazed (it will be lined with plastic so it does not matter if it is porous). Wire mesh lies across the top, on to which a layer of marbles is placed. The fountain container is filled with shingle to support the fountainhead and displace the water.

The pump draws water up from the reservoir and pushes it out of the fountainhead, the fountain pot fills and overflows, and the water runs back down to feed the reservoir. When the pump is switched off, the water ceases flowing and gradually trickles back to the reservoir. You may choose any shape of container, as long as the size is such that there is always slightly more water in the reservoir than in the fountain container. The copper goldfish will slowly age to an attractive, irridescent blue-green.

## YOU WILL NEED

### Materials
for a fountain 520 mm in diameter and 315 mm high
- Ceramic container for main reservoir: about 520 mm in diameter and 180 mm deep
- Plastic pond liner: 900 mm long and 900 mm wide (allows for cutting waste)
- Small submersible pump
- Flexible armoured plastic pipe: long enough to protect the pump cable
- Electricity circuit breaker
- Fountainhead: with extension tube to fit your pump
- Roll of masking tape
- Flowerpot: about 200 mm in diameter and 130 mm deep
- Galvanized 6 mm wire mesh: 600 mm long and 600 mm wide (allows for cutting waste)

- Ceramic container for fountain: about 320 mm in diameter and 180 mm deep with a hole in the bottom
- Shingle (small): half a bucketful of washed shingle
- Copper sheet: 150 mm square and 1 mm thick
- Marbles: 100 glass marbles in assorted colours and sizes

### Tools
- Tape measure and a piece of chalk
- Scissors: to cut the plastic
- Knife
- Wire snips
- Pliers
- Scissors: heavy-duty scissors to cut the copper sheet

## Step-by-step: Making the mini marble fountain

*Liner*
*If the liner is dirty, wash*
*it before you begin*

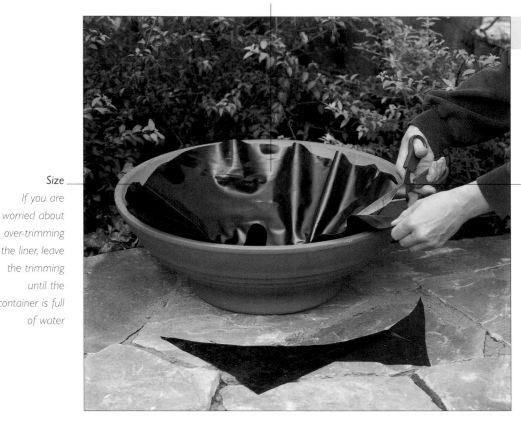

*Size*
*If you are*
*worried about*
*over-trimming*
*the liner, leave*
*the trimming*
*until the*
*container is full*
*of water*

**1** Take the reservoir container and use the tape measure, chalk, scissors and knife to trim the pond liner to fit. It should cover the inside of the bowl to within 10 mm of the rim.

*Trimming*
*Cut off the*
*excess liner*
*10 mm below*
*the rim*

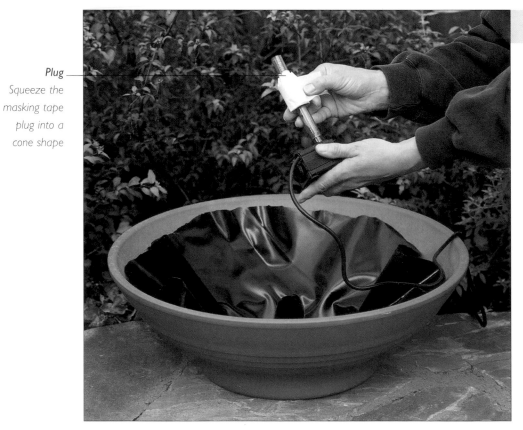

*Plug*
*Squeeze the*
*masking tape*
*plug into a*
*cone shape*

**2** Put the pump in the bottom of the bowl, making sure that the cable is protected by the armoured pipe and the electricity circuit breaker. Fit the fountainhead extension tube to the pump, wrapping masking tape around the tube to make a pliable, cone-shaped plug.

### *Helpful hint*

The cone-shaped plug of masking tape doesn't need to be a watertight fit in the hole, only tight enough to hold the tube in place and to ensure that the top bowl is always topped up – so that the water overflows.

*Mesh size*
*Choose the smallest mesh
size that you can find*

*Folded edge*
*Fold over the
edge of the
mesh using
the pliers*

**3** Set the flowerpot upside-down over the pump, pushing the cone-shaped plug of the extension tube through the drainage hole. Use the wire snips and pliers to shape the galvanized mesh into a large disc that fits over the reservoir pot. The fountainhead extension tube pokes through the mesh. The disc should be supported at its centre by the flowerpot, and at its rim by the reservoir pot.

*Centre hole*
*Cut a hole in
the mesh so
that it fits over
the plug*

*Fountainhead*
*Pack the shingle tightly
around the head*

*Copper sheet*
*Choose thin copper that
can be cut easily*

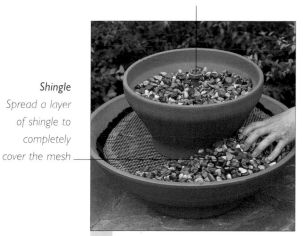

*Shingle*
*Spread a layer
of shingle to
completely
cover the mesh*

*Scissors*
*Use heavy-duty
scissors to cut
the copper*

*Sharp edges*
*Be careful not
to cut your
fingers on the
sharp edges*

**4** Put the fountain container on the upturned flowerpot and wire mesh, fitting the fountainhead on the extension tube, and top up the pot with shingle. Cover the wire mesh with a thin layer of shingle, so the plastic liner cannot be seen.

**5** Draw the goldfish on the copper sheet and cut them out with the heavy-duty scissors. Scatter the marbles and fish over the shingle in both of the containers. Fill the reservoir container with water, and switch on the power.

# Romantic fountain

There are at least four reasons to install a traditional romantic fountain in your pond: you can appreciate the beauty of the fountain statuette, the sound of the water is delightful, the oxygenated water is good for the pond life and, best of all, the whole thing can be set up in a morning and running by the afternoon.

**TIME**

One day (a couple of hours to sort out the pump and the fountain, and the rest of the day to complete).

**SAFETY**

Ask a helper to watch over you while you are bridged over the pond – just in case!

## YOU WILL NEED

**Materials** *for a statuette 430 mm high in a pond 475 mm deep*
- Rubber mat: about 450 mm long and 300 mm wide (or to suit your plinth)
- Bricks: sufficient to bring the top of the plinth level with surface of the water
- Concrete or ceramic pot with a hole in the base to use as a plinth: 400 mm high
- Submersible pump: a large pump to suit the height of your statuette
- Fountainhead: with connections to fit both the statuette and the pump

- Flexible armoured plastic pipe: long enough to protect the full length of the pump cable
- Electricity circuit breaker
- Fountain statuette: 430 mm high, made from concrete, stone or fibreglass

**Tools**
- Extension ladder: long enough to bridge pond
- Plank: long and narrow enough to fit the ladder
- Steel tape measure

## A DELIGHTFUL SPRAY OF WATER

Decide how best to bridge your pond with the ladder (you lie across it in order to install the fountain without getting into the pond yourself) and how to ensure that the ladder is both stable and secure. Calculate the number of bricks needed to bring the plinth up to the surface level of the water. Work out how you are going to site the pump under the plinth, with the power cable running back to the mains, and with the outlet tube of the pump running up through the hole in the plinth to the connection on the underside of your statuette. Plan the route of the cable so that it can be hidden as it exits the pond. Gather the various components together on land and have a dry-run fitting before you go near the water.

CROSS-SECTION OF THE FOUNTAIN

Fountainhead
*Carefully chosen to fit the link-up joint on the statuette*

Statuette
*430 mm high
Made from cast concrete*

Connector
*Joint linking the pump to fountain*

Concrete or ceramic pot
*400 mm high with a hole in the base*

Rubber mat
*450 mm long and 300 mm wide*

Brick      Liner      Pump

Armoured pipe
*To protect power cable*

# Step-by-step: Making the romantic fountain

*Plank*
*Use a plank to distribute your weight*

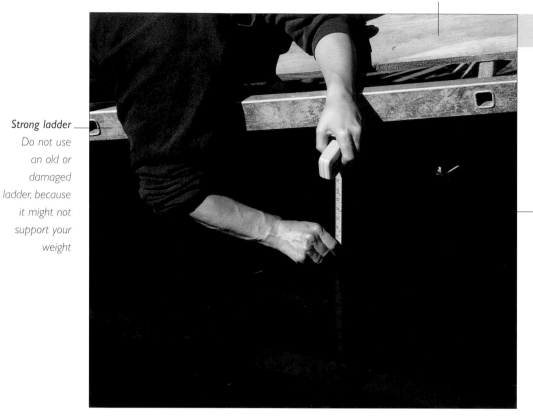

*Strong ladder*
*Do not use an old or damaged ladder, because it might not support your weight*

1 Bridge the water with the ladder and the plank, to allow you to work in reasonable comfort over the centre of the pond. Lower the tape measure into the pond to find out the depth of the water (the distance between the pond liner and the surface of the water).

*Tape measure*
*For an accurate reading, keep the tape measure vertical*

*Height*
*Raise the statuette to a height where it sits on the surface of the water*

2 Have a trial run to assess how many bricks will be required. Spread the rubber mat on the lawn, and start positioning the bricks to take the full weight of the concrete plinth. Build up the bricks until you raise the top of the plinth to be level with the surface of the water.

### Helpful hint

The size and weight of the plinth relate to the size of the sculpture. If the plinth is very weighty, you may need to set up two ladders, so a friend can help. The plinth will have to be pushed across one of the planks.

*Be careful*
Do not drop the bricks into place,
as they will damage the pond liner

*Pump setting*
If the pump has flow controls, turn these
to full and adjust later if necessary

*Brick
foundation*
Arrange the
bricks to make
a broad base
for the plinth

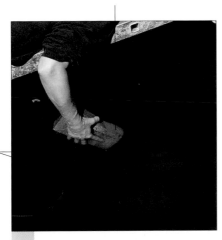

*Clean
rubber mat*
Wash the
mat before
use to avoid
contaminating
the pond

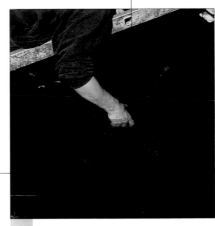

*Safety*
Disconnect the
pump while
you are in
contact with
the water

**3** When you are satisfied with the trial
run, move the whole arrangement
into the pond. Start by setting the bricks
on the rubber mat, laying them around a
space for the pump. Make sure that every
brick is stable. You might need small
wedges of tile or slate to adjust the height
of the bricks. Put the plinth on to check.

**4** Put the pump on the mat, encircled
by the bricks, and carefully fit the
fountainhead connecting tube. Slide the
armoured plastic pipe over the electric
cable and fit the electricity circuit breaker.
Remove your hands from the water, ask a
helper to switch on the power, and check
that the pump is working.

*Pipe position*
Ease the pipe up and
through the hole

*Ageing*
If you like, brush a little milk on the
statuette to encourage algae to form

*Connecting*
Connect the
flexible tube to
the pipe in
the statuette

*Be careful*
Avoid holding
the statuette at
a fragile point

*Plinth*
Carefully lower
the plinth over
the pump

**5** Switch off the power. Position the
plinth so that the pump is fully
enclosed, with the extension tube running
up through the central hole in the plinth.
Repeat the checking procedure.

**6** Fit the connecting tube to the
statuette, and place the statuette
squarely on the plinth, making sure that
it is level. Finally, rerun the checking
procedure to make sure that you have
not dislodged the pump.

# French millstone bell fountain

This is a wonderfully tranquil feature to have in a garden. The central French millstone, out of which water wells up into a bell shape, is reminiscent of cobbled courtyards in Provence, bubbling spring waters, and times past. This particular design, which incorporates a surrounding ring of shingle and stones, also draws inspiration from traditional Japanese gardens.

### TIME

Half a day (three hours to dig the hole and arrange the bricks and stones, and an hour to bury the power cable and fine-tune the fountain).

### SAFETY

The millstone is heavy, so protect your hands with gloves and get help with the lifting.

## YOU WILL NEED

**Materials** *for a millstone fountain 1.25 m in diameter*
- Bricks: about 20 house bricks – enough to edge a circle 1.25 m in diameter
- Sand: a wheelbarrow load
- Sump: a preformed plastic liner about 660 mm in diameter, with a lid to fit
- Small submersible pump
- Fountainhead with a telescopic extension tube
- Flexible armoured plastic pipe: long enough to protect the full length of pump cable

- Electricity circuit breaker
- Millstone: a concrete disc about 400 mm in diameter and 100 mm thick
- Shingle (medium): 50 kg
- Pebbles and cobbles: 25 kg
- Stone: a single carefully chosen "guardian" stone
- Rockery plants

**Tools**
- Tape measure and string line
- Spade
- Wheelbarrow
- Spirit level

### CROSS-SECTION OF THE FRENCH MILLSTONE FOUNTAIN

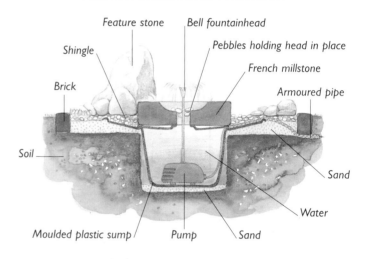

Feature stone · Bell fountainhead · Shingle · Pebbles holding head in place · Brick · French millstone · Armoured pipe · Soil · Sand · Water · Moulded plastic sump · Pump · Sand

### PLAN VIEW OF THE FRENCH MILLSTONE FOUNTAIN

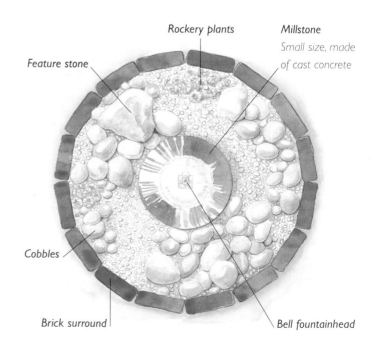

Rockery plants · Millstone *Small size, made of cast concrete* · Feature stone · Cobbles · Brick surround · Bell fountainhead

## A BUBBLING FRENCH SPRING

The working action of this fountain is beautifully simple – the pump pushes water up through the fountainhead, it falls in a bell shape on the millstone and the surrounding stones, and then flows back into the sump. The diameter of the sump you purchase must be greater than that of the millstone, and the pump must be powerful enough to push the water up through the thickness of the millstone and on through the fountainhead.

The good thing about this project is that (apart from concealing the power cable) it can be fitted directly into the middle of a lawn without much upset. The telescopic extension tube for the fountainhead is a clever item: you simply adjust the length of the tube to suit the thickness of the millstone and your design features. If you need to create more height with extra cobbles around the fountain, you just lengthen the tube to fit. When selecting the pump, measure the distance between the level of the water in the sump and the top of the millstone, then get a pump that is powerful enough to do the job.

## Step-by-step: Making the French millstone bell fountain

*Structure*
*The moulded pattern of the surround channels the water into the sump*

*Sand*
*Spread an even layer of sand over the earth*

*Sump brim*
*Has to catch all the water from the fountain, to channel it back to the pump. The bigger the pump, the more spray is created, and the wider the diameter of the sump brim needs to be*

**1** Use the tape measure and string line to scribe out a circle 1.25 m in diameter. Dig out the whole area to the depth of the brick edge. Dig a hole in the centre deep enough for the sump, plus 50 mm (for the sand). Edge the circle with bricks. Cover the area between the brick edge and the hole for the sump with a layer of sand 50 mm deep.

*Sump lid*
*Slide the lid over the pump outlet pipe and locate it on the surround*

**2** Place the sump in the hole and bed the rim in the sand. Arrange the pump (connecting the extension tube and fountainhead), protect the full length of the cable with the armoured pipe, install the electricity circuit breaker and make sure that it is operational.

### *Helpful hint*

If the pump fails to work, or the impeller bearing feels gritty when you turn it round by hand, the water is probably contaminated with sand. Wash the pump under running water, clean out the sump and change the water.

*Fountainhead*
*Make sure the head is vertical*

**3** After sliding the sump lid in place, so that the pump is protected and concealed, carefully lift the millstone into position. Check with the spirit level that the millstone is true and, if necessary, make adjustments with slivers of rock and sand.

*Positioning*
*Measure from the brick edging to the edge of the millstone, to check the millstone is centred*

*Levelling*
*If necessary, use small wedges of stone to level up the millstone*

**4** Spread shingle over the sand and the sump lid, and centre the fountainhead within the millstone by packing it with pebbles. Finally, decorate the area with the guardian stone, cobbles and rockery plants.

*Fountainhead*
*Pack stone around the fountainhead to centre it in the millstone*

*Pebbles and cobbles*
*Use different sizes of stone to create contrast*

# Weeping hypertufa boulder

Hypertufa emerged in the 1940s in response to a craze for using old stone sinks as plant troughs. Enthusiasts were inspired to disguise glazed white kitchen sinks with a mixture of sphagnum moss, sand and cement – known as hypertufa – to make them look like stone. If you would like to create a weird and wonderful water feature, rather like a friendly alien life-form, a weeping hypertufa boulder is hard to beat!

| TIME |
| --- |
| Two weekends (two days to cast the boulder, five days for the hypertufa to cure, and two more days for excavating the boulder, digging the sump and fixing the pump). |

| SAFETY |
| --- |
| This project involves a lot of strenuous digging and heaving, so you will need a willing helper. |

## YOU WILL NEED

**Materials** *for a boulder 500 mm high and 450 mm in diameter*

- Soft copper pipe: 900 mm long, 10 mm in diameter
- Hypertufa mix: 1 part (25 kg) cement, 1 part (25 kg) sharp sand, 4 parts (100 kg) sphagnum moss
- Sump: a preformed plastic sump about 660 mm in diameter, with a lid to fit
- Medium-size submersible pump
- Flexible armoured plastic pipe: long enough to protect the full length of the pump cable
- Electricity circuit breaker
- Sand: 100 kg (for bedding the slabs)
- Paving slabs: 4 cast concrete slabs about 450 mm square; a single paving slab 300 mm square

- Plastic tube: 500 mm long, 10 mm in diameter, with hose clips to fit (to link the copper pipe to the pump)
- Stone with a hole through to fit your boulder recess
- Cobbles: 25 kg
- Shingle (medium): 50 kg
- Stones: carefully chosen feature stones, size and shape to suit

**Tools**

- Tape measure and a piece of chalk
- Spade
- Wheelbarrow
- Garden trowel
- Shovel
- Tamping beam: 400 x 80 x 50 mm
- Rope
- Electric drill with a 25 mm masonry bit
- Spirit level
- Screwdriver

## WEIRD BOULDER

Find an area of uncultivated ground for casting the boulder. Ideally, it needs to be well drained and made up of a mixture of heavy loam and clay. The boulder is cast upside-down, with the copper tube cast in place, and the "weep" hole is set in a hollow. All the hollows in the surface of the finished boulder start out as bumps on the sides of the hole, therefore the copper tube is inserted into a bump towards the bottom of the hole. The finished boulder weighs something over 150 kg, so it is quite a problem to get it out of the ground. One easy way is to dig a ramp down to the bottom of the cast hole – like a flight of shallow steps – and then loop a rope around the boulder and drag it out in stages.

## CROSS-SECTION OF THE WEEPING HYPERTUFA BOULDER

Stone
With a hole through

Copper pipe

Hose clip

Cobbles

Shingle

Soil level

Sand

Large paving slab
*450 mm square, bedded on sand and propped with pieces of broken slab to make it slope slightly towards the central small paving slab*

Small paving slab
*300 mm square
Hole drilled in centre*

Armoured pipe

Soil

Plastic tube

Moulded plastic sump

Water

Pump

Sand

# Weeping hypertufa boulder

## CROSS-SECTION OF THE SOIL MOULD AND BOULDER

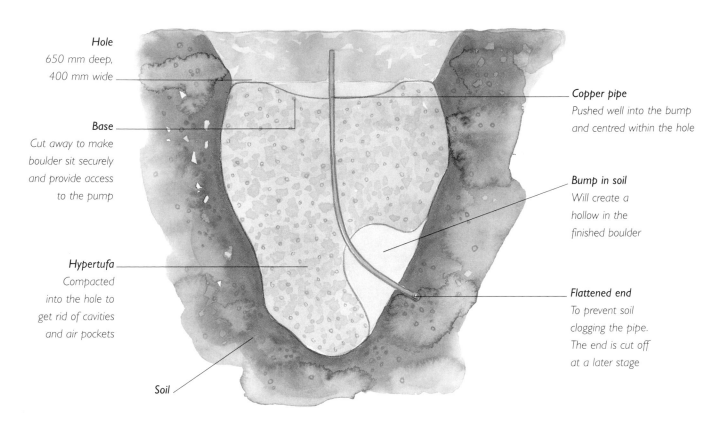

*Hole*
650 mm deep,
400 mm wide

*Base*
Cut away to make
boulder sit securely
and provide access
to the pump

*Hypertufa*
Compacted
into the hole to
get rid of cavities
and air pockets

*Soil*

*Copper pipe*
Pushed well into the bump
and centred within the hole

*Bump in soil*
Will create a
hollow in the
finished boulder

*Flattened end*
To prevent soil
clogging the pipe.
The end is cut off
at a later stage

## CROSS-SECTION SHOWING EXCAVATION

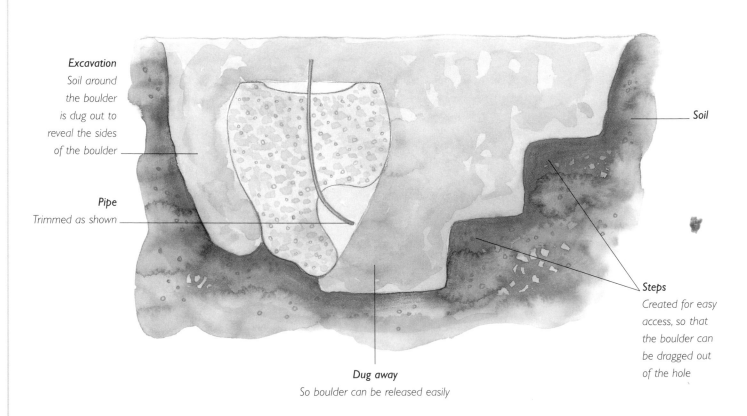

*Excavation*
Soil around
the boulder
is dug out to
reveal the sides
of the boulder

*Pipe*
Trimmed as shown

*Soil*

*Steps*
Created for easy
access, so that
the boulder can
be dragged out
of the hole

*Dug away*
So boulder can be released easily

SIDE VIEW OF THE BOULDER

**Positioning**
Boulder placed so that the water outlet is in view

**Stone with a hole through it**
Can be a found stone, or one that has been drilled. Placed over the water outlet pipe

**Cobbles and large stones**
Arranged around the boulder

**Boulder**
Connected to the pump centred underneath it

PLAN VIEW SHOWING THE ARRANGEMENT OF THE PAVING SLABS

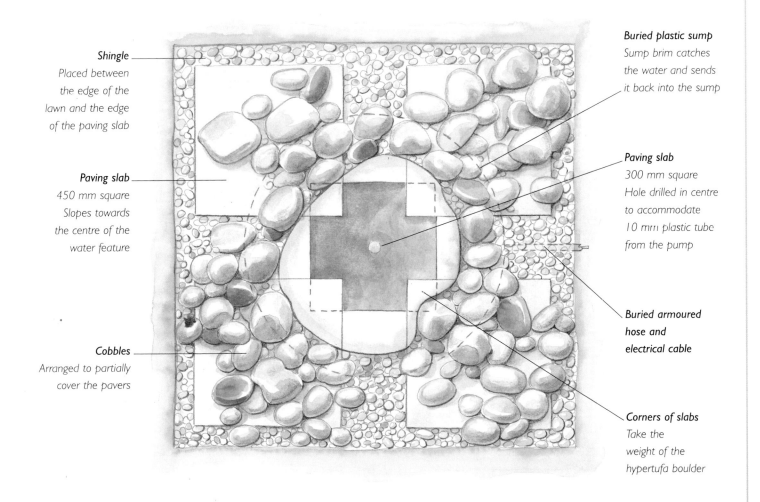

**Shingle**
Placed between the edge of the lawn and the edge of the paving slab

**Buried plastic sump**
Sump brim catches the water and sends it back into the sump

**Paving slab**
450 mm square
Slopes towards the centre of the water feature

**Paving slab**
300 mm square
Hole drilled in centre to accommodate 10 mm plastic tube from the pump

**Cobbles**
Arranged to partially cover the pavers

**Buried armoured hose and electrical cable**

**Corners of slabs**
Take the weight of the hypertufa boulder

# Step-by-step: Making the weeping hypertufa boulder

*Rim*
*Excavate under the rim to create*
*a boulder that narrows at its base*

*Modelling*
*The hole starts as a cylindrical space. The rim is then undercut so that the girth of the hole is greater than the rim size. Bumps and indentations on the sides of the hole help the boulder to look more realistic*

*Bump*
*The size of the bump will equal the size of the pocket in the boulder*

**I** Use the spade and garden trowel to carefully excavate the casting hole, making it about 650 mm deep and 450 mm wide. Dig the hole so that it bulges out at the centre and narrows towards the bottom. Model a bump on the side wall, towards the bottom of the hole.

*Copper tube*
*Bend the tube so that it hooks into the bump*

*Bump*
*The bump will hold its shape better in damp soil or clay soil. If your soil disintegrates, use a plastic container to form the bump*

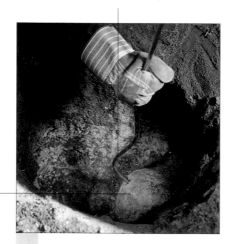

**2** Flatten one end of the soft copper pipe and push 50 mm of the pipe into the modelled bump (flattened end first). Centre the rest of the pipe within the hole.

*Tamping*
*Gently tap the hypertufa mix until water rises to the surface*

*Air pockets*
*Make sure that you eliminate air pockets and fill all the gaps*

**3** Add water to the hypertufa ingredients to create a mix with a soft consistency. Shovel the hypertufa, little by little, into the hole, tamping it down with the beam so that it completely fills the hole and there are no air pockets.

*Trowel work*
*Gradually excavate around the boulder*

*Careful handling*
*Lower the slab gently to avoid breaking the sump*

*Sand*
*Lay a generous bed of sand around the sump*

*Surrounding slabs*
*Position each large slab so the corner lies on the centre slab. Check with the spirit level. Prop the outer edge with pieces of broken slab so it slopes slightly towards the centre slab*

*Steps*
*Dig a flight of steps to run down to the bottom of the boulder*

*Centre slab*
*Place the slab on the sump lid and pull the plastic tube through*

**4** Wait four or five days for the hypertufa to cure, then use the spade and shovel to dig a flight of steps down to the bottom of the cast. Use the trowel to excavate around the form. Cut a hollow around the copper inlet pipe. With the rope, drag the cast boulder out of the hole and clean off any earth.

**5** Set up the sump and pump, with armoured pipe and electricity circuit breaker, as described in step 2 of the French millstone bell fountain project on page 54. Surround with sand. Drill a hole through the centre of the 300 mm slab. Connect the plastic tube to the pump and run it through the drilled slab. Arrange the other four slabs.

*Copper inlet pipe*
*Trim the end of the pipe to leave about 40 mm sticking out of the bottom*

*Connecting tube*
*Slide the plastic tube on to the copper inlet pipe*

**6** Use the hose clips and screwdriver to link the plastic tube to the copper pipe on the underside of the boulder, and then carefully centre the boulder on the slabs. Cut off the flattened portion of the copper pipe protruding from the recess and place the stone with the hole over the end. Decorate the area with shingle and stones.

*Helpful hint*

Be careful not to break off the delivery end of the copper pipe when moving the boulder. However, if you do, carefully excavate the bottom of the boulder to reveal more pipe.

# Wine bottle spray fountain

**Moving water and glass are a magical combination. There is something uplifting, almost spiritual, about the way that the water catches the sunlight as it sprays over the glass, and collects in the hollows in the bottles to make tiny pools. Moreover, this project is eco-friendly, because it recycles glass.**

| TIME |
|---|
| A day (four hours to dig the hole and arrange the bottles, and the rest of the time to bury the power cable and fine-tune the fountain). |

| SAFETY |
|---|
| The bottle circle is heavy, so handle it with care. Wear goggles when moving it. |

## YOU WILL NEED

**Materials** *for a fountain 910 mm in diameter*
- Sump: a sheet of plastic about 1.66 m in diameter (large enough to be pushed down into the hole with a generous overlap all round)
- Small submersible pump
- Flexible armoured plastic pipe: long enough to protect the full length of pump cable
- Electricity circuit breaker
- Pavers: 4 cast concrete slab segments to go around a hole 450 mm in diameter
- Fountainhead: with a telescopic extension tube to fit the pump

- Plastic rainwater pipe: 300 mm long and 80 mm in diameter
- Wine bottles: about 20 with a dimple in the bottom, in various colours
- Strong, waterproof sticky tape): 1 roll
- Bricks: 4 bricks
- Small cobbles and shingle: 12 kg of each
- Plastic carrier bags for infill: 4 bags
- Large cobbles: 25 kg

**Tools**
- Tape measure
- String line
- Spade

## BOTTLE-BOTTOMS UP

This project is unusual because the decorative containment – the area around the fountainhead nozzle – is made from a clutch of upturned traditional wine bottles. The clever thing about gathering together groups of circular-section items of the same diameter, such as pipes, pencils or wine bottles, is that they automatically want to form a circle. However, you do have to begin with a circle of the same size at the centre.

Starting from the centre point, the number of circles or bottles always doubles for each consecutive ring – six in the first ring, twelve in the second ring, 24 in the third, and so on. So if you want to make a much larger arrangement than the one shown here, you just keep collecting bottles and alter the diameter of the circle to suit. The advantage of traditional wine bottles is that the dip in their base, when they are upturned, catches the water. We have used a concrete tile circle to surround the circle of bottles, but you could substitute bricks, cobbles, or whatever you wish.

CROSS-SECTION OF THE WINE
BOTTLE SPRAY FOUNTAIN

Fountainhead
Fitted with a spray nozzle

Plastic infill
Crinkled-up plastic bags to hold fountain extension tube in centre of pipe

Paver
Holds the plastic sheet in place

Armoured pipe

Water level

Channel
Under lawn

Small cobbles and shingle
Arranged around the bottles

Soil

Brick
Placed to support the bottles

Plastic rainwater pipe

Pump

Sump
Plastic sheet

# Wine bottle spray fountain

PLAN VIEW OF THE WINE BOTTLE SPRAY FOUNTAIN

**Fountainhead**
*Held in place with crumpled plastic
bags and topped with small pebbles*

**Joint**
*Packed with sand*

**Concrete paver**
*4 segments to fit round bottle circle*

**Upturned bottle**
*Dip collects water*

**Cobbles**
*Packed around bottles
to hold them in place*

**Paver circle**
*910 mm in diameter*

**Bottle circle**
*450 mm in diameter*

**Plastic rainwater pipe**
*300 mm long, 80 mm in diameter
Centred within the bottle ring*

## CUT-AWAY VIEW OF THE WINE BOTTLE SPRAY FOUNTAIN

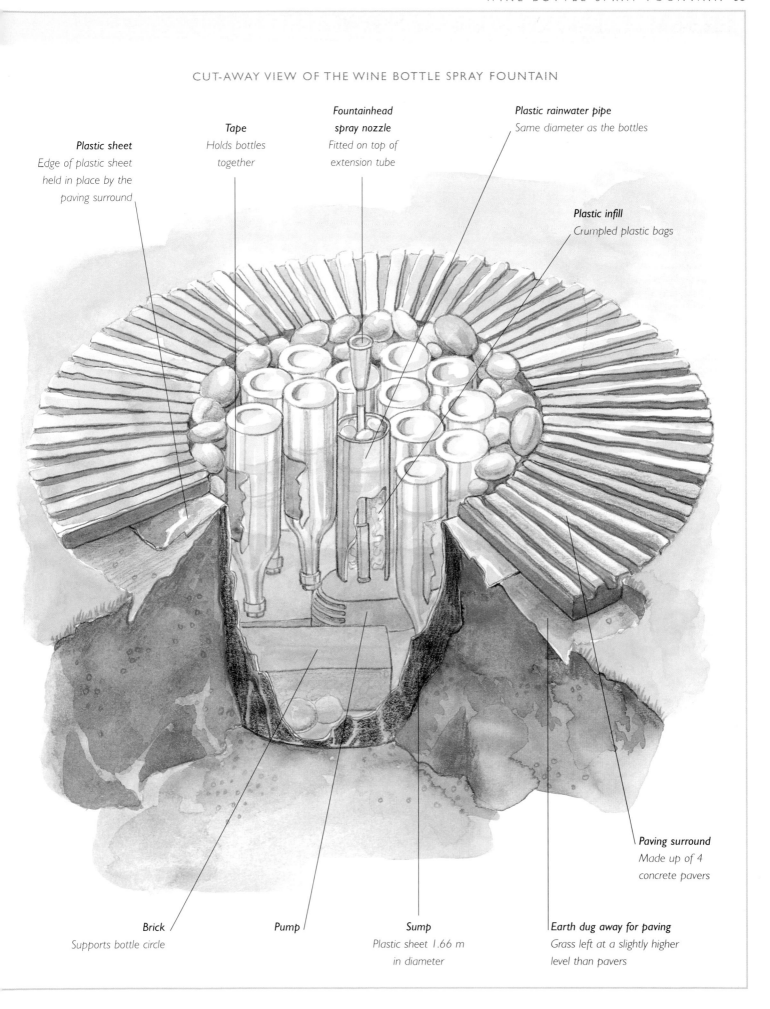

**Plastic sheet**
Edge of plastic sheet
held in place by the
paving surround

**Tape**
Holds bottles
together

**Fountainhead
spray nozzle**
Fitted on top of
extension tube

**Plastic rainwater pipe**
Same diameter as the bottles

**Plastic infill**
Crumpled plastic bags

**Paving surround**
Made up of 4
concrete pavers

**Brick**
Supports bottle circle

**Pump**

**Sump**
Plastic sheet 1.66 m
in diameter

**Earth dug away for paving**
Grass left at a slightly higher
level than pavers

## Step-by-step: **Making the wine bottle spray fountain**

*Plastic surround*
*Pull the plastic sheet out and over the edge
of the hole to make a drainage apron*

**I** Draw out a circle on the ground for the sump hole, using the tape measure and string line. Make it 450 mm in diameter. Cut back the turf and dig out the hole to a depth of 400 mm. Line the hole with the plastic sheet and put in the pump, complete with the fountainhead extension tube. Slide the pump cable down the armoured pipe and dig out a channel to run it below the level of the lawn. Fit the electricity circuit breaker.

*Pump*
*Sit the pump on the bottom of the sump and push on the telescopic extension tube*

*Testing the pump*
*Test the pump after every fitting stage, but stand back from the pump and water while the power is on*

*Positioning*
*Set the tile segment in place while keeping the plastic in position*

*Bottle size*
*Choose bottles of more or less the same diameter*

*Handling*
*The tile segments are fragile, so lay them with care*

*Rainwater pipe*
*Diameter is 80 mm – similar to that of the bottles*

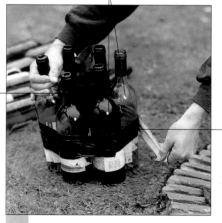

*Waterproof tape*
*Strap the inner ring of bottles with tape*

**2** Lay the four tile segments so that they encircle the sump hole and hold the plastic sheet securely in place. Connect the fountainhead to the extension tube, and switch on the power to check that everything is working.

**3** Take the length of rainwater pipe, ring it with six wine bottles standing upright, and then bind the whole thing together with the waterproof tape.

*Outer ring of bottles*
*Make sure the bottles fit together well*

*Be careful*
*The bottles are heavy, so take care when lifting*

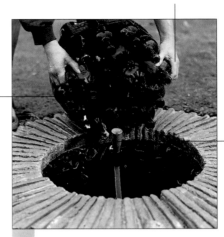

*Waterproof tape*
*Strap the tape round the bottles several times until it all feels firm*

*Testing*
*Before you turn the bottles over, make sure each bottle is held firmly*

*Fountainhead*
*Positioned to go through the rainwater pipe in the centre of the bottle circle*

**4** Group twelve more wine bottles around the initial six-bottle core, and strap them together with waterproof tape. Continue with the strapping until the whole arrangement is secure.

**5** Very carefully, turn the wine bottle arrangement over, and lower it in place over the fountainhead and pump. You might need to put a few bricks in the sump hole to bring the bottles up to the correct height. Fill the spaces around the bottles with small cobbles and shingle.

*Cobbles*
*Use cobbles for decoration and as a way of stopping garden debris from getting into the sump hole*

*Centring*
*Use pebbles to centre the fountainhead in the pipe*

*Adjusting*
*Adjust the position of the bottles by wedging pebbles around the edge*

**6** Push plastic bags into the rainwater pipe to centre the fountainhead, and top up with small cobbles. Finally, fill the sump with water and position cobbles around the arrangement. Switch on the pump and adjust the fountainhead for best effect.

### *Helpful hint*

If you want to take the project one step further, you could have the wine bottles set at different heights, with a coloured uplighter lamp installed in the sump to illuminate the bottles and the fountain.

# Japanese deer scarer

The Japanese *shishi-odoshi* or deer scarer is amazingly good fun, and very popular with children and dogs alike! Water trickles from a delivery pipe into an upturned spout, a see-saw tips the water back into the pond, the end of the see-saw falls back on the striker stone with a heavy "clunk", and the procedure starts over again.

**TIME**

A weekend (about twelve hours for the woodwork, and four hours for setting it up and fixing the pump).

**SAFETY**

Bamboo is very spiky – watch out for razor-sharp edges and splinters.

## YOU WILL NEED

**Materials** *for a deer scarer 1 m in diameter*
- Bamboo: one piece 2 m long and 60 mm in diameter (for see-saw and delivery pipe), and one piece 4 m long and 120 mm in diameter (for main post and support posts)
- Plastic tube: 5 m long and 10 mm in diameter (to link delivery pipe to pump), with hose clips to fit
- Medium-size submersible pump
- Flexible armoured plastic pipe: long enough to protect the full length of the pump cable

- Electricity circuit breaker
- Striker stone

**Tools**
- Tape measure, pencil and black felt-tip marker
- Coping saw
- Knife: one or more sharp knives
- Electric drill with a 20 mm woodworking bit
- Rod: a length of wooden dowel or metal rod about 900 mm long (to pierce the inner membranes of the bamboo)
- Club hammer
- Spade
- Garden hosepipe

## ACHIEVING A BALANCE

The first hurdle in this project is finding a supplier for the bamboo. We discovered two sources – one was the local garden centre, and the other advertised in a specialist garden magazine. When you have obtained the bamboo, walk round your garden and consider the various siting options. For example, are you going to have the deer scarer set up over an existing pond – so that the water routes from the pond, through the bamboo, and then back into the pond? Or are you going to provide the deer scarer with its own self-contained sump?

The water delivery pipe also needs to be arranged so that the input end is hidden from view. That is not a problem if the ground slopes steeply down to the pond, because the input end can easily be hidden away in a convenient shrub or rock, with the rest of the pipe being supported by the two bridge uprights. If, however, your ground is level, one option is to build a pile of rocks or logs, or a little hut, to provide a support and cover for the input.

SIDE VIEW DETAIL OF MAIN POST (CROSS-SECTION)

*Main pivot pin*

*Pierced membrane*

*Main post*

FRONT VIEW DETAIL OF MAIN POST

*Cut-away window*

*Main pivot pin*

*Locking pin*

*See-saw*

*Main post*

PLAN VIEW DETAIL OF MAIN POST

*Spliced spout*

*See-saw*

*Main post*

# Japanese deer scarer

### CROSS-SECTION OF THE JAPANESE DEER SCARER

**Large bush**
Conceals hose and the other support post

**U-shaped stirrup**
Supports delivery pipe

**Bamboo delivery pipe**
1.2 m x 60 mm
Conceals plastic tube carrying water

**Dividing membranes in bamboo**
Pierced using rod

**Spout**
Placed so that the water falls into the see-saw pipe

**Plastic tube**
Carries water

**Support post**
1.2 m x 120 mm Bamboo

**Main post**
1.1 m x 120 mm
Bamboo

**Window**
70 mm wide x 170 mm deep
Base of window 130 mm above ground level

**See-saw**
580 mm x 60 mm
Bamboo. Spout to pivot 270 mm, pivot to end 310 mm

**Pivot pin**
Centred in window

**Membrane**
First membrane pierced with rod

**Water in pond**
Reservoir for pump

**Plastic pipe**
Water supply

**Striker stone**
Chosen for size and character

**Pump**

**Power cable in armoured plastic pipe**
Hidden well below ground

**Hardcore**
Compacted around the base of the post

**Tile**
To provide a firm footing for the bamboo post

**Soil**

**Pond liner**

**Sand**

## PLAN VIEW OF THE JAPANESE DEER SCARER

**Bamboo delivery pipe**
*Hollowed out. Conceals plastic tube with water supply*

**Support post**
*Hidden in bush*

**Support post**

**Pond**

**Plastic tube**
*Buried about 300 mm deep. Free from sharp bends and kinks*

**See-saw spout**
*Placed so that the water is returned to the reservoir pond*

**Pump**

**Striker stone**

**Buried power cable**
*In armoured plastic pipe*

**See-saw**

**Main post**

## Step-by-step: Making the Japanese deer scarer

*Grip*
*Hold the bamboo at the top to minimize movement and make sawing easier*

*Blade position*
*Swivel the blade so that the teeth are aligned with the cut*

*Waste area*
*Mark the waste to be sawn away*

**1** Cut a 1.1 m length of 120 mm bamboo for the main post. Use the tape measure, pencil and felt-tip marker to clearly mark the size and position of the two "windows" on the main post for the see-saw — one on each side. The windows are 70 mm wide and 170 mm deep, and the base of each should be about 130 mm above ground level when the post is in position. Carefully cut away the waste with the coping saw. Mark the hole for the pivot pin.

*Carving*
*Carve the pin to make a decorative "knuckle" at the end*

**2** Cut a 580 mm length of the 60 mm bamboo for the see-saw pipe. With the knife, carve a pivot pin out of a bamboo offcut. Make it 200 mm long and 15 mm wide apart from a "knuckle" at one end. Drill a 20 mm hole for the pivot pin through the main post (lining it up with the centre of the window) and 270 mm in from the spout end of the see-saw. Trim the pivot to fit.

*Knife control*
*Brace your thumb against the bamboo so you have greater control over the knife*

*Locking pin*
*The pin needs to be a*
*tight fit in the pivot*

*Window*
*Trim the hole if*
*necessary so*
*that the see-*
*saw can move*
*unhindered*

*Pivot hole*
*Make the pivot*
*hole with the*
*point of a knife*

*Finishing*
*Use the knife to scrape the*
*edges to a smooth finish*

*Shaping*
*Round over*
*all the sharp*
*edges and*
*corners*

*Added strength*
*Note that the*
*naturally*
*occurring plate*
*strengthens the*
*joint at the end*

**3** Set the see-saw in the main post, slide the pivot in place, and then cut and whittle a locking pin (from a bamboo offcut) to hold the pivot in position. Use the rod to pierce the membrane in the front end of the see-saw.

**4** Cut a 1.2 m length of the 120 mm bamboo and split it down the middle to make the two support posts. Use the coping saw and knife to make the U-shaped stirrup detail at the top of each post. Cut the bamboo delivery pipe to 1.2 m long and use the rod to pierce the membranes in the middle of the bamboo.

*Testing*
*Use the garden hosepipe to test out the*
*best position for the delivery pipe*

*Mounting*
*Dig a hole for*
*the main post.*
*Tap hardcore*
*around its base*
*with the club*
*hammer to*
*hold the*
*post firm*

*Striker stone*
*Position the*
*striker stone for*
*the loudest and*
*best-sounding*
*"clunk"*

**5** Mount the main post, then use a garden hosepipe, with water running through it, to help decide where the bamboo delivery pipe should be sited in order for water to pour into the see-saw. Use the plastic tube (where possible, buried 300 mm underground) and the hose clips to link the bamboo water delivery pipe to the pump in the bottom of the pond. Protect the power cable from the pump with armoured pipe (also buried underground) and use an electricity circuit breaker.

## Inspirations: Bamboo water features

Japanese gardens are designed to be oases of tranquillity, suitable for reflection and meditation. A deer scarer, filling up with water, gently tilting and pouring, accompanied by the regular beat of bamboo upon stone, seems to represent the inexorable nature of time. There is something truly wonderful about watching the water and the machine working in harmony to produce a rhythm that symbolizes the importance of balance in the natural world.

ABOVE A Japanese deer scarer in action at the Chelsea Flower Show, England. This low-rise version features short bamboo pipes and a large striker stone.

RIGHT If you like the idea of having a Japanese feature, but want something easier to make than a deer scarer, you could build a *tsukubai*. This has a

bamboo pipe supplying water to a pot, which overflows and runs into the gravel, where it is channelled and pumped back up through the bamboo spout.

# Perpetual water tap

This is a project that will keep people guessing! Water flows from the tap, hour after hour, apparently being allowed to run to waste. Those with a wicked sense of humour will find it great fun to observe visitors' faces when they notice it. The perpetual stream of water is a very successful illusion, and you will find that most people are compelled to turn the tap off, and to berate you for wasting water.

## TIME

A weekend (eight hours for the copperwork plumbing, and eight hours for digging the sump and setting up the pump).

## SAFETY

Cut copper and clipped wire mesh are both difficult to hold, with lots of splinters of copper and sharp, jagged edges, so be sure to wear goggles and leather gloves.

## YOU WILL NEED

**Materials** *for a perpetual water tap 1 m high and 700 mm in diameter*
- Plastic bucket (for the sump)
- Medium-size submersible pump
- Flexible armoured plastic pipe: long enough to protect the full length of the pump cable
- Electricity circuit breaker
- Natural wooden post: treated with wood preserver, and with bark removed, 1.1 m long
- Tap: brass or copper wall-mounted tap (old or new)
- Copper water pipe: 1.2 m long, 15 mm in diameter
- Compression elbow: 2 copper compression corner joints to fit the pipe
- Copper tap bracket: bracket wall plate with screw thread to fit the tap, a compression joint to fit the pipe, with screw to fix it to the post

- Copper saddle clip: 15 mm with screws to fit
- Hardcore: 1 bucketful
- Slates or tiles (waste pieces)
- Plastic tube: 500 mm long and 15 mm in diameter (to link copper pipe to pump), with hose clips to fit
- Natural border log roll: 2 m long, 300 mm high
- Plastic sheet: a circle about 1 m in diameter
- Galvanized 6 mm wire mesh: 600 mm square (allows for cutting waste)
- Cobbles: 25 kg

**Tools**
- Wheelbarrow
- Spade
- Tape measure
- Log saw
- Screwdriver
- Pipe cutter: large enough to cut the copper pipe
- Adjustable spanner
- Bucket: for hardcore
- Club hammer
- Scissors
- Wire snips

CROSS-SECTION OF THE PERPETUAL WATER TAP

Tap attached to post

Treated post

Copper water pipe

Plastic sheet
*Butts up to logs*

Copper saddle clip

Cobbles

Log roll border

Compression elbow joint

Power cable in armoured pipe

Soil

Plastic tube

Hose clip

Plastic bucket

Pump    Water    Hardcore    Slates or tiles
*To create firm base*

## WATER ON TAP

The perpetual water tap is an ingenious project: once the pump is running, the tap appears to have been left on. The quaint brass tap, with the understated wooden post and the log roll surrounding fence, suggest that the whole set-up is old. Visit car boot sales and fleamarkets to search out a tap that has character, and that can be wall mounted. Ours dates from the 1920s, and probably comes from an old bath boiler. Clean the tap with metal polish and remove the washer. Because the perpetual water tap is self-contained, with its own integral sump and pump, it can be sited just about anywhere in the garden. However, to consolidate the illusion of a functional tap, choose a spot where you might conceivably want a water supply – perhaps in the corner of an orchard, or by the garden door, or in a courtyard.

# Perpetual water tap

PLAN VIEW OF THE PERPETUAL WATER TAP

**Copper water pipe**
*1.2 m long, 15 mm in diameter*
*Descends into reservoir*

**Tap**
*Attached to bracket –*
*design to suit chosen tap*

**Post**
*1.1 m long, bark removed and*
*treated with wood preserver*

**Cobbles**
*Carefully placed*
*to hold the plastic*
*sheet in position*

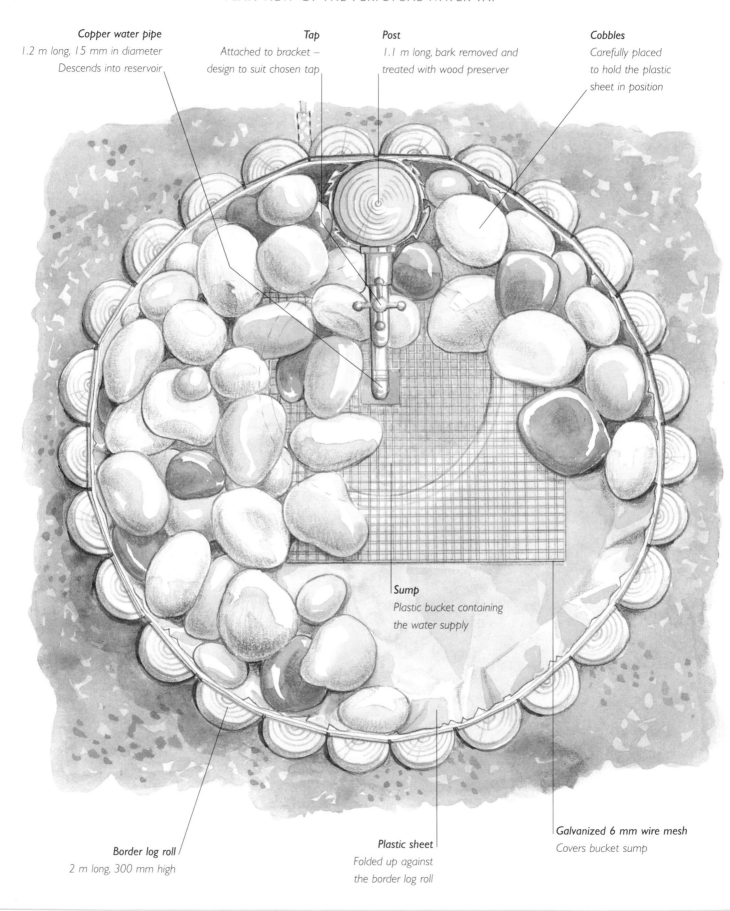

**Sump**
*Plastic bucket containing*
*the water supply*

**Border log roll**
*2 m long, 300 mm high*

**Plastic sheet**
*Folded up against*
*the border log roll*

**Galvanized 6 mm wire mesh**
*Covers bucket sump*

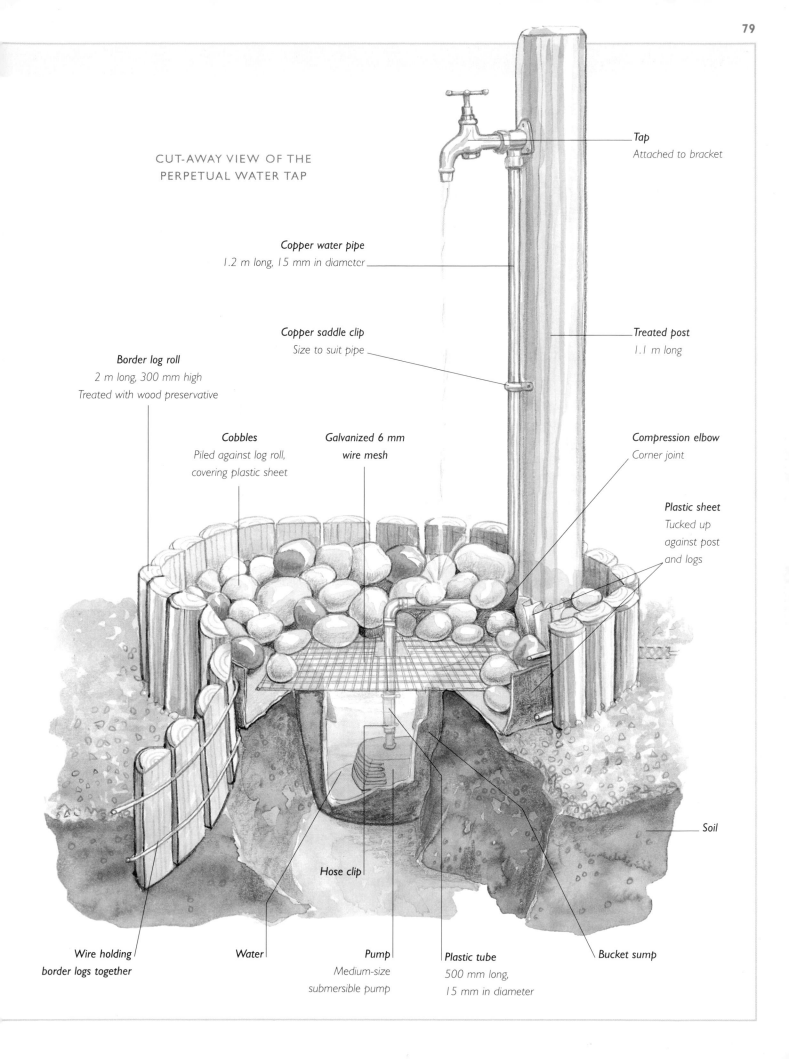

CUT-AWAY VIEW OF THE
PERPETUAL WATER TAP

**Tap**
*Attached to bracket*

**Copper water pipe**
*1.2 m long, 15 mm in diameter*

**Treated post**
*1.1 m long*

**Copper saddle clip**
*Size to suit pipe*

**Border log roll**
*2 m long, 300 mm high*
*Treated with wood preservative*

**Cobbles**
*Piled against log roll,*
*covering plastic sheet*

**Galvanized 6 mm**
**wire mesh**

**Compression elbow**
*Corner joint*

**Plastic sheet**
*Tucked up*
*against post*
*and logs*

**Soil**

**Wire holding**
**border logs together**

**Water**

**Pump**
*Medium-size*
*submersible pump*

**Hose clip**

**Plastic tube**
*500 mm long,*
*15 mm in diameter*

**Bucket sump**

## Step-by-step: **Making the perpetual water tap**

*Spade*
*Use a small spade for digging clay soil*

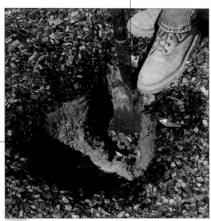

*Stones*
*Make sure that you remove any sharp stones*

*Pump*
*Test the pump after every fitting stage*

*Cable protection*
*Protect the cable with armoured pipe*

*Handle*
*Leave the bucket handle attached until the last moment*

**1** Use the spade to dig a hole wide and deep enough to hold the plastic bucket. When the bucket is in place, the rim should be flush with the ground. The bucket must not be jammed in place – it should fit easily into the hole. Level the bucket with pieces of stone if necessary.

**2** Clean the bucket and position the pump in it, fitting the cable with armoured pipe and an electricity circuit breaker. Fill the bucket with water. Switch on the power and check that the pump is working. (Pumps can be fickle – keep testing them during construction.)

*Copper saddle clip*
*Bridge over the copper water pipe and screw in place*

*Bark*
*Scrape the bark off the post*

*Joints*
*Avoid over-tightening the plumbing joints*

*Pipe position*
*Ensure that the pipe is centralized in the bucket*

*Fixing the post*
*Bang hardcore around the post until it is firm and stable*

**3** Measure and cut the post to size with the log saw. Use the pipe cutter to cut the pipe lengths, join the pieces of pipe with the compression elbow joints (but do not fully tighten the joints) and fit the tap bracket and tap. Fix the pipe and tap bracket to the post using saddle clips and screws, and tighten the compression joints with the spanner.

**4** Set the post in the ground, placing it on tiles to broaden the base of the post and prevent it forcing itself into the ground. The inflow end of the copper pipe goes into the bucket. Put broken hardcore around the post and beat it down with the club hammer. Link the pump to the copper pipe by means of the plastic tube.

*Arranging the plastic*
*Spread out the plastic and ease*
*it up the side of the log roll*

*Outlet hole*
*Cut a hole in*
*the mesh for*
*the pipe to*
*slide through*

**5** Surround the bucket sump with the border log roll, making an enclosed well. Cover the well with the plastic sheet, cutting a cross in the middle so it flaps into the bucket. Cover the plastic with the wire mesh. Trim the plastic (with the scissors) and the mesh (with the snips) so that they fit within the well.

## Helpful hint

If you want to have a larger tap and a greater flow of water, you will require a bigger apron of plastic sheet, so that the increased spray of water is directed back into the sump.

*Cobble*
*covering*
*Pile cobbles*
*inside the log*
*surround until*
*the mesh*
*is completely*
*concealed*

**6** Fill the well with cobbles, concealing the plastic and the mesh completely. Finally, fill the bucket with water, switch on the power, and turn on the tap.

*Post support*
*The cobbles*
*around the*
*post give it*
*extra support*

# Copper cascade

This project is ideal if you have a modern garden and want a contemporary water feature to complement it. It is also perfect if you would simply like to try your hand at a copper and wood sculpture. Made from a railway sleeper and copper sheet, water trickles out of a copper tube, into copper cups, and back to the pond.

**TIME**

A weekend (eight hours for cutting and shaping the copper, four hours for mounting the sleeper, and four hours for connecting the water).

**SAFETY**

The weight of the sleeper is back-breaking – don't try moving it without help.

## YOU WILL NEED

**Materials** *for a cascade 1.3 m high*
- Copper sheet: 1 x 430 mm long, 260 mm wide, 1 mm thick; 1 x 330 mm long, 250 mm wide, 1 mm thick; and 1 x 230 mm long, 150 mm wide, 1 mm thick
- Railway sleeper: 2 m long, 260 mm wide, 160 mm thick
- Galvanized coach bolts: 3 x 50 mm long and 20 mm in diameter, suitable for fixing field gate hinges
- Soft copper pipe: 2 m long and 10 mm in diameter
- Plastic tube: 500 mm long and 10 mm in diameter (to link the copper pipe to the pump), and hose clips to fit
- Medium-size submersible pump
- Flexible armoured plastic pipe: long enough to protect the full length of the pump cable
- Electricity circuit breaker
- Plastic sheet: about 900 mm long and 400 mm wide

- Cobbles: 25 kg
- Shingle (medium): 50 kg
- Rocks: a selection of feature rocks

**Tools**
- Thick rope to make handles for moving the sleeper: 4 m
- Blowlamp: plumber's gas blowlamp
- Tape measure and a piece of chalk
- Electric drill with long-reach 20 mm bit
- Metal snips: a pair of metalworker's tin snips large enough to cut the copper sheet
- Claw hammer
- Adjustable spanner
- Spade
- Pipe cutter: a plumber's pipe cutter large enough to cut the 10 mm pipe

CROSS-SECTION
OF THE
COPPER CASCADE

*Soft copper pipe*
*For water supply from pump cascade*

*Copper cascade*

*Plastic sheet*
*Lining area of cascade*

*Plastic tube*

*Pump*  *Sand*  *Soil*

*Railway sleeper*
*Chosen for size and character*

*Galvanized coach bolt*

*Buried power cable to pump*
*Protected with flexible armoured plastic pipe*

*Buried part of railway sleeper*

*Hardcore*
*Compacted around base*

*Slate or tile*
*To provide a firm footing*

## RUNNING WATER AND GOLDEN COPPER

The first thing to take into consideration is the weight of the railway sleeper. Though it is undoubtedly heavy – at least 200 kg – we found that we could drag it around the garden with a couple of short lengths of thick rope. With the sleeper set flat on the ground, the lifting procedure is simple. All you do is loop a rope around each end of the sleeper, so that you have two handles, then move it with a lot of very small lifts.

Ideally, the sleeper needs to be positioned over a pond or pool, so that the water flow-off can run back as a little brook. Cutting the copper sheet is hard work, but your supplier may be able to clip it to shape first. The copper needs to be softened before it can be cut. A blowlamp is used to heat the copper until it turns red, then it is plunged into cold water. Next, make your cuts. After a few minutes, you may need to repeat the heating and plunging process, because cutting makes the copper go hard again.

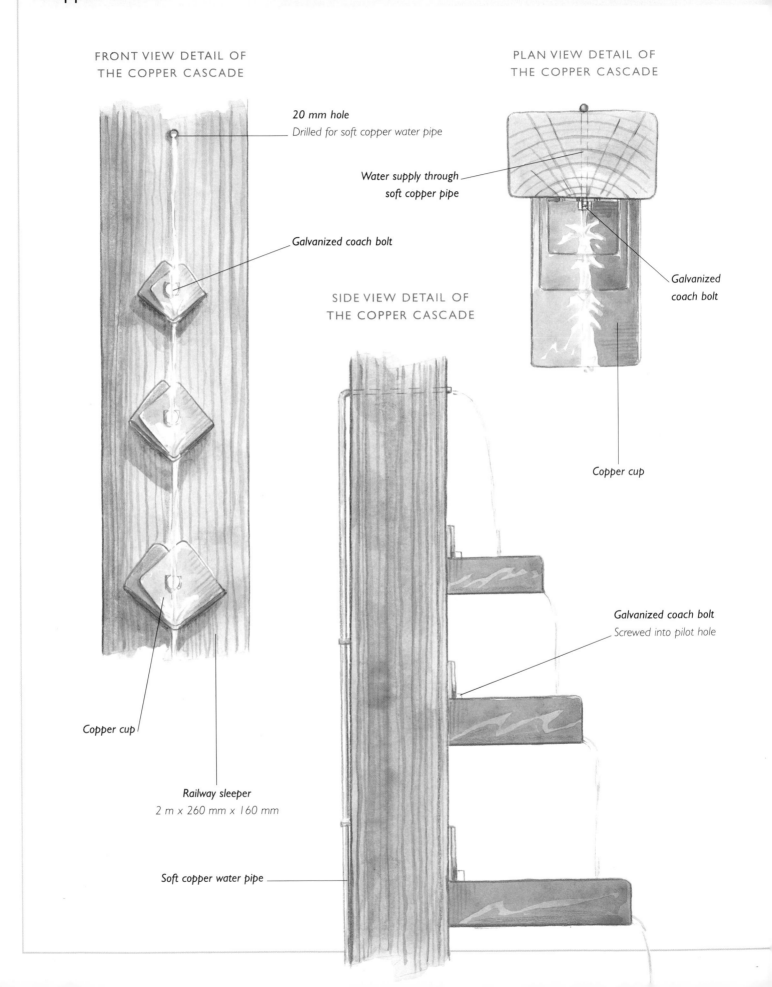

# Copper cascade

FRONT VIEW DETAIL OF
THE COPPER CASCADE

PLAN VIEW DETAIL OF
THE COPPER CASCADE

**20 mm hole**
*Drilled for soft copper water pipe*

*Water supply through
soft copper pipe*

*Galvanized coach bolt*

SIDE VIEW DETAIL OF
THE COPPER CASCADE

*Galvanized
coach bolt*

*Copper cup*

*Copper cup*

*Galvanized coach bolt*
*Screwed into pilot hole*

*Copper cup*

*Railway sleeper*
*2 m x 260 mm x 160 mm*

*Soft copper water pipe*

## CUTTING PLANS FOR THE COPPER CUPS

*Crossed diagonals*
*Fix centre point*

Cutting line

Cross fold line

Central fold line

**Top cup**
*230 x 150 mm*

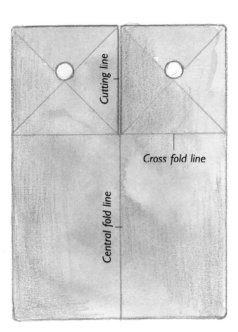

Cutting line

Cross fold line

Central fold line

**Middle cup**
*330 x 250 mm*

*Holes*
*20 mm holes drilled*
*slightly above centre point*

Cutting line

Cross fold line

Central fold line

**Bottom cup**
*430 x 260 mm*

## FOLDING STAGES TO MAKE THE COPPER CUPS

**Stage 1**
*Round off the corners.*
*Fold over lengthwise to*
*make a straight gulley*

**Stage 2**
*Fold in one flap*
*until it is at right*
*angles to the*
*base of the cup*

**Stage 3**
*Fold in the other flap so it is*
*at right angles to the base.*
*Align the holes for the bolt*

## Step-by-step: Making the copper cascade

*Trimming corners*
*Cut off the sharp corners*
*to make them rounded*

*Rounded corners*
*Aim for a slightly*
*rounded corner*

*Fold line*
*Run the cut*
*just up to*
*the chalked*
*central fold line*

*Hardening*
*The hammering*
*will harden the*
*copper and*
*it may need to*
*be reheated*

*Hammer work*
*Work with*
*lots of small,*
*tapping strokes*

**1** To make a copper cup, soften the copper sheet with the blowlamp and plunge it into cold water. Use the tape measure and chalk to draw out the design on it. Drill the two 20 mm holes. Use the metal snips to cut down the central fold line to the cross fold line.

**2** Bend the copper along the central fold line. Rest it on the railway sleeper – using it like an anvil – and, with the claw hammer, gently tap the copper over the angle. Fold and tap the flaps in the same way, aligning the drilled holes.

*Copper colour*
*The heat of the blowlamp removes the protective*
*grease and creates a bronze-like surface*

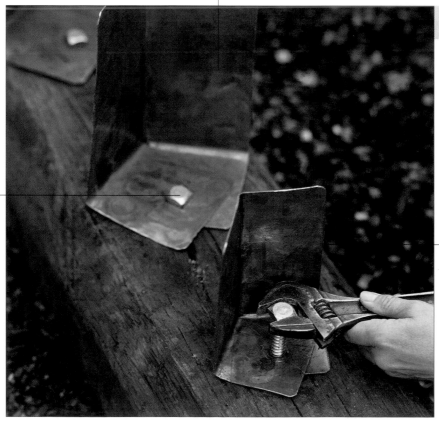

**3** Drill the five 20 mm holes in the railway sleeper – two holes for the water pipe, and the other three holes for the bolts. Use the coach bolts and adjustable spanner to fix the three copper cups in place.

*Fixing the*
*copper*
*Keep the*
*copper units*
*upright as*
*you tighten*
*the bolts*

*Safety*
*Be careful*
*not to cut*
*your hands on*
*the edge of*
*the copper*

*Digging*
*Dig a hole just big enough*
*to take the sleeper*

*Bending the copper*
*Avoid creating sharp bends, which*
*will cause the pipe to collapse*

*Pipe position*
*Shape the*
*pipe so that it*
*runs parallel*
*with the back*
*of the sleeper*

*Adjusting*
*the pipe*
*Adjust the pipe*
*so that the*
*water falls into*
*the first cup*

**4** Dig a hole for the sleeper (when the sleeper is in place at the edge of the pond, the bottom copper cup should be about 150 mm clear of the ground). Stand the sleeper upright in the hole and firm the earth around it.

**5** Run the soft copper pipe from the pond, through the bottom sleeper hole, up the back of the sleeper, and then back through the top of the sleeper. Cut it to length with the pipe cutter, so that it exits like a little tap just above the top copper cup. Avoid sharp bends in the pipe.

*Stones*
*Reduce soil erosion by putting*
*stones under the falling water*

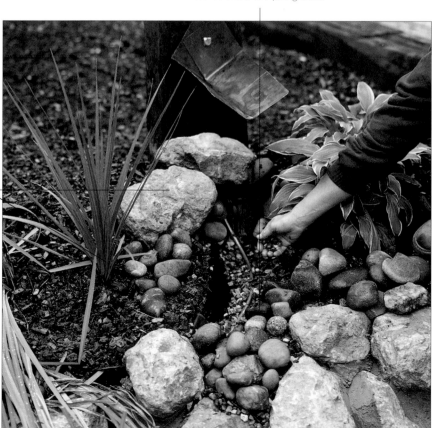

*Stones*
*and plants*
*Arrange plants*
*and stones to*
*give the feel*
*of a natural*
*stream*

**6** Run the input end of the copper pipe into the pond and link it to the pump with the plastic tube. Slide the armoured pipe in place over the cable, install and check the electricity circuit breaker. Use the plastic sheet, cobbles, shingle and rocks to cover the copper pipe and to create a stream or dry bed effect.

*Helpful hint*

If you want to swiftly age the copper and give it a rich green patina, repeatedly heat it up with a blowlamp and brush it with salt, several weeks before using it in the project.

# Woodland grotto

In many country areas, there are traditional folktales describing the pixies, goblins and sprites who inhabit secret woodland dells, pools and rocky places. If you suspect that there are little people living at the end of your garden, and you would like to build them a mini grotto surrounded by greenery (or you simply want to build a home for your garden's frogs and toads), this is the project for you!

### TIME

A weekend (four hours to dig the sump, four hours to set up the base stones, and another eight hours for the rest of the stonework and for fixing the pump).

### SAFETY

Make sure that children do not walk on the mesh covering the sump hole, just in case they fall in.

## YOU WILL NEED

**Materials** *for a grotto 900 mm high and 750 mm in diameter*
- Plastic bucket (for sump)
- Medium-size submersible pump to suit height of grotto, with extension pipe
- Flexible armoured plastic pipe: long enough to protect the full length of pump cable
- Electricity circuit breaker
- Plastic sheet: 1 m square
- Galvanized wire mesh: 400 mm square
- Limestone slab: about 600 mm square and 50 mm thick

- Mortar: 2 parts (100 kg) cement, 1 part (50 kg) lime, 9 parts (450 kg) soft sand
- Large limestone boulders: about 25, 200–300 mm in diameter
- Small pieces of broken paving slab for cascade: 2 or 3 pieces
- Shingle (medium to large): 25 kg
- Cobbles: 25 kg (100 mm and bigger)
- Rocks: 7 medium size

**Tools**
- Wheelbarrow
- Spade
- Scissors
- Pointing trowel

## A QUIET PLACE

The inspiration behind this project was a Druid spring that we saw near a village in deepest Somerset, in the south-west of England. It was beautifully situated in a wooded dell well away from the village – a wonderfully quiet and tranquil spot.

The mission of our woodland grotto is the creation of a garden space that is given over to rest and meditation – a sort of coming together of a Japanese water garden, a natural spring, and a clearing in the forest. Once you have studied the designs, think about a possible site. Ideally, it needs to be wooded, with lots of lush green vegetation, and above all, it should be quiet. If you can find a place in dappled shade, which is quite wild, with lots of moss, rotting bark and wood beetles, this would be ideal. The only other thing that needs to be taken into consideration is how to run the water and electricity supplies to the spot.

CROSS-SECTION OF THE WOODLAND GROTTO

Limestone boulders
*Mortared together*

Water supply pipe from pump

Limestone paving slab

Galvanized wire mesh

Plastic sheet
*Cut so the water falls into the bucket*

Pump extension pipe
*Lies in channel*

Buried armoured plastic pipe
*Protects the power cable*

Bucket
Sump

Pump

Soil

Water

# Woodland grotto

PLAN VIEW OF THE WOODLAND GROTTO

**Large limestone boulders**
*200–300 mm in diameter*
*Used for foundation of the grotto*

**Pump extension pipe**
*For water supply. Runs from the
pump, out of the sump along a
channel under the limestone slab,
and up the back of the grotto*

**Cascade**
*Made from
small broken
paving slabs*

**Buried power
cable in
armoured pipe**

**Cobbles**
*Chosen and placed
for best effect*

**Galvanized wire mesh**
*Centred over the bucket*

**Limestone slab**
*600 x 600 x 50 mm*
*Placed on ground alongside sump,
lapping over it. Pump extension pipe
lies in channel underneath it*

**Sump**
*Bucket containing
water and pump*

**Medium-size rocks**
*Arranged on
the ground*

**Plastic sheet**
*Slopes towards bucket*

CUT-AWAY VIEW OF THE WOODLAND GROTTO

**Roof stone**
*A wide, flat stone, positioned to span the walls of the grotto*

**Key boulder**
*Set in a generous amount of mortar*

**Mortar**

**Cascade**
*Stones placed to achieve best effect*

**Water**
*From pump extension tube*

**Woodchips**
*Spread over surrounding ground*

**Limestone paving slab**
*Bridging the bucket*

**Sump**
*Bucket containing water and pump*

**Galvanized wire mesh**
*To support cobbles and stone*

**Plastic sheet**

## Step-by-step: Making the woodland grotto

*Pump extension pipe*
*Make sure that the extension*
*pipe is set in a channel*

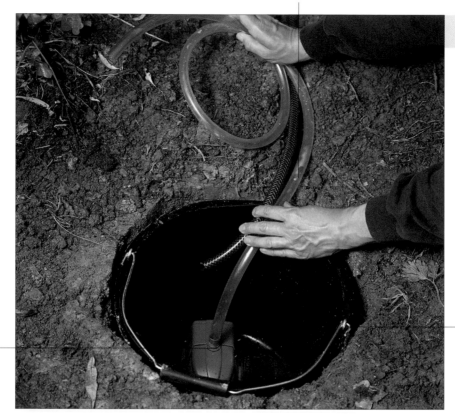

**1** Dig a hole deep enough to hold the plastic bucket for the sump, so that it lies with its rim level with the ground. Set the pump in the bucket, complete with armoured pipe over the cable. Fit the electricity circuit breaker. Fix the extension pipe in the pump, and dig a channel in the ground for it to lie in.

*Handle*
*Remove the*
*bucket handle*
*prior to*
*spreading the*
*plastic sheet*

*Pump*
*Test the pump*
*after every*
*fitting stage*

*Mortar*
*Be generous*
*with the mortar*
*around the first*
*ring of boulders*

**2** Cover the bucket sump with the plastic sheet. Cut a 100 mm slot in the sheet with the scissors, so that all the water from the outlet pipe is bound to flow back into the bucket. Place the limestone slab so that it laps over one end of the sump, and use the mortar and pointing trowel to start building a C-shaped ring of limestone boulders on the slab.

### *Helpful hint*

If the weather is hot and sunny, you will need to spray the boulders with water just prior to bedding them in the mortar.

*Extension pipe*
Set the pipe so that the water
dribbles on to the centre of the slab

*Key boulder*
Position the top boulder
for best effect

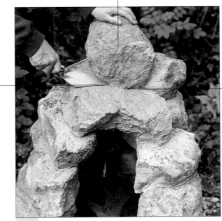

*Mortar*
Build the
second ring of
boulders when
the first layer of
mortar has
begun to stiffen

*Modelling*
Use the point
of the trowel
to clean up
and shape the
mortar

*Extra mortar*
If necessary,
add mortar
to joints that
look empty

**3** Build a second course of boulders. Run the extension pipe from the back of the grotto and over the ring of boulders to the front, so that the water dribbles on to the centre of the slab. Position the small pieces of broken paving slab to make a cascade.

**4** Build two more courses of boulders. Leave until the mortar is part-cured. Sit the final key boulder in place on top of the heap and use the pointing trowel to tidy up the mortar. Add additional smaller boulders as you think fit.

*Texturing*
Tap the semi-cured mortar with the tip of
the trowel to give it a weathered effect

**5** Clean out any grit from inside the sump and cover the top with the mesh. Push the mesh under the front edge of the slab. Finally, cover the plastic sheet and mesh with shingle, and decorate the whole site with cobbles and rocks. You could group stones to resemble a shrine, add personal artefacts, or include plants or driftwood.

*Decorating*
Arrange
cobbles around
the base of
the grotto

*Ornament*
If you want to,
place a brass
toad or small
concrete
statuette inside
the grotto

# Copper spiral spray

In action, this project is similar to a wind sculpture, where eddies of wind set a wooden spiral in motion. The copper spiral works in much the same way, the only real difference being that water supplies the motive force. The "fun" part of the project, which may test your patience, is adjusting the force and flow of the water.

## YOU WILL NEED

**Materials** *for a spiral spray 1.23 m high, 1.3 m long and 880 mm wide*
- Railway sleepers: 260 mm wide and 160 mm thick – 1 x 1.23 m long, 2 x 1.3 m long, 2 x 880 mm long, 2 x 780 mm long, and 2 x 360 mm long
- Woodchips: 8 wheelbarrow loads
- Plastic pond liner: 1.42 m long and 1 m wide (allows for cutting waste)
- Medium-size submersible pump
- Flexible armoured plastic pipe: long enough to protect the full length of pump cable
- Electricity circuit breaker
- Hard copper water pipe (as used by plumbers): 1.8 m long, 15 mm in diameter
- Galvanized nails: 30 flat-headed nails, 60 mm long
- Soft, pliable copper pipe (as used by gas fitters): 1.9 m long and 10 mm in diameter
- Plastic tube: 200 mm long and 10 mm in diameter (to link the soft copper tube to the pump), with hose clips to fit
- Copper sheet: 350 mm square, 0.05 mm thick (soft and thin enough to cut with tin snips)
- Strong nylon fishing line: 500 mm long, with a spinner joint to fit

**Tools**
- Tape measure and a piece of chalk
- Log saw
- Spade
- Garden trowel
- Spirit level
- Scissors: to cut the plastic
- Claw hammer
- Brace: a carpenter's brace with a 20 mm auger bit
- Pipe cutter: a plumber's pipe cutter large enough to cut the 10 mm pipe
- Metal snips: a pair of metalworker's tin snips large enough to cut the copper sheet

## TRICKLING AND TURNING

Part of the fascination of this project is that it is made up from lots of component parts, rather like a large building kit, so putting it together is very satisfying. Watching the spiral spin, and the sight and sound of moving water, are the chief pleasures of the copper spiral spray, so this will affect whereabouts you decide to site it in your garden. Do you want it close by so that you can watch every little ripple as the water plays over the copper? Or would you prefer to view it from a distance?

The actual making procedures are all straightforward, apart from sawing the wood, which requires some effort. It's best to buy a brand new log saw with a pack of blades. To guard your back, make sure that you do the sawing at a height that is comfortable. Do not stoop or overreach. You also need to think about how you are going to manoeuvre the weighty sleepers around the garden.

### CROSS-SECTION SIDE VIEW

Soft copper pipe
*Bent to shape*

Anti-twist device
*Spinner joint*

Copper spiral

Water pipe
from pump

Cobbles
*Cover the plastic and the pump*

Pump

Support strut
*Hard copper pipe fixed with nails*

Plastic sheet
*Spread across base and up against side of the sleepers*

Buried power cable in armoured pipe

# Copper spiral spray

PLAN VIEW OF THE COPPER SPIRAL SPRAY

Power cable

Support strut
*1.2 m x 15 mm
Hard copper pipe
nailed in place*

Cobbles
*Conceal the pump
and the plastic sheet*

Copper spiral
*Tied to copper outlet
pipe so it hangs under
the falling water*

Railway sleeper
*1.23 m x 260 mm x 160 mm*

Hole
*20 mm hole drilled 150 mm
down from top of post*

Soft copper pipe
*Delivers the water*

Anti-twist device
*Spinner joint from
fishing tackle shop*

Copper spiral
*Cut from copper sheet*

Support strut
*1.2 m long
Hard copper pipe*

Railway sleepers
*Set so that the
rounded, weathered
face is uppermost*

Hole
*20 mm hole drilled 510 mm
down from top of post*

Water pipe from the pump
*Soft copper pipe*

FRONT VIEW OF THE
COPPER SPIRAL SPRAY

SIDE VIEW OF THE COPPER SPIRAL SPRAY

**Hole**
20 mm hole drilled 150 mm
down from top of post

**Soft copper pipe**
Bent to spout shape

**Anti-twist device**
Spinner joint. Prevents the
thread from knotting up

**Hole**
20 mm hole drilled 510 mm
down from top of post

**Copper spiral**
Stretched so that it
channels the water

**Support strut**
1.2 m x 15 mm
Hard copper pipe
nailed in place

**Water pipe from pump**
Soft copper pipe

**Railway sleepers**
Form the retaining walls to hold the
water. Placed with rounded face
uppermost. Fixed together with nailed
300 mm strips of hard copper pipe

**Buried power cable
in armoured pipe**

**COPPER
SPIRAL DESIGN**

**Copper sheet**
350 mm square, 0.05 mm thick
Cut into circle 300 mm in diameter

**Centre point of circle**

# Step-by-step: Making the copper spiral spray

**Corner joint**
*Butt the sleepers together to make a 90° corner*

Use the tape measure and chalk to mark out the railway sleepers, then cut them to size with the log saw. Lay out the first course of sleepers on the ground, and use the spade and garden trowel to pack them with earth or woodchips so that they are level. Check with the spirit level.

**Levelling**
*Use the spirit level to check that the sleepers are well placed*

**Packing out**
*Lever up the sleepers with a spade and fill any cavities with woodchips*

**Plastic sheet**
*Allow a generous overlap of plastic, at least half-way across the sleeper*

**Corners**
*Fold the plastic at the corners to improve the appearance*

**2** Cover the sleepers with the plastic pond liner, creating a shallow pool. Set the pump in place, together with the armoured pipe to cover the cable. Fit the electricity circuit breaker. Fill the pool with water. Trim the plastic with the scissors.

**Copper straps**
*Sleepers held together with straps fixed with flat-headed galvanized nails*

**Corner joint**
*Set the second layer so that the vertical joints are staggered*

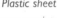

**Plastic sheet**
*Ensure that the plastic sheet is trapped between the sleepers*

**3** Lay the second course of sleepers on top of the first, sandwiching the plastic sheet and holding it secure. Use the claw hammer to flatten strips of hard copper pipe into straps to lap over the joints and hold the structure together.

*Nailing*
*Use at least two nails at each end of the bracket*

*Spout*
*Make a generously curved spout*

*Vertical post*
*Check that the post is held straight while you fix both brackets*

*Bending*
*You will need to bend the pipe in a wide curve to get it through the second hole*

*Pushing angle*
*As you push the pipe through, keep it at 90° to the post*

**4** Set the vertical post in position at one end of the pool, make checks with the spirit level, and then fix it in place at the back and sides with lengths of hard copper pipe. Use as many galvanized nails as you think necessary.

**5** Use the brace and auger bit to drill two holes, 20 mm in diameter, through the sleeper. Cut the soft copper pipe to length with the pipe cutter. Connect the plastic tube to the copper pipe and the pump. Slide the copper pipe into place, running it from the pump, through and up the sleeper, and out of the top hole, creating a spout over the pool.

*Spinner joint*
*The spinner prevents the line from twisting and breaking*

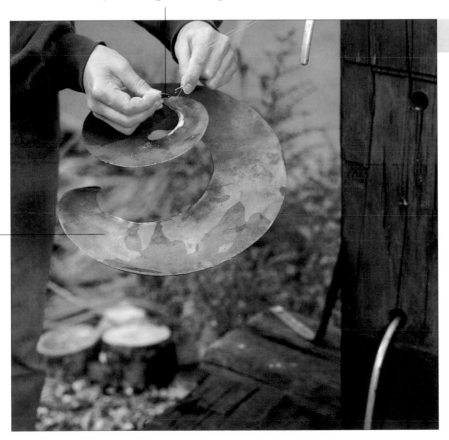

**6** Cut the copper spiral out of the copper sheet with the metal snips, and hang it from the spout by means of the fishing line and the spinner joint. Position the spiral so that the falling water sets it in motion.

### Helpful hint

If you want to reduce costs for this project, you could use recycled copper to make the copper spiral. A salvaged water tank would be suitable, provided that the copper is thin enough to cut easily. Try looking at your local amenity tip, or visit a scrap metal dealer.

*Copper spiral*
*Adjust the extension of the spiral under a trickle of water until it starts to spin satisfactorily*

# Glass waterfall

Glass bricks are a winning design feature in their own right, but if you add some

decorative copperwork and a waterfall spray, you have something really special. If

you live in a townhouse with a small courtyard, and have a passion for minimalism –

lots of white walls, glass and flat surfaces – this project will appeal to you.

**TIME**

Two weekends (eight hours for the copperwork, eight hours for siting the pump, and the remaining time for completion).

**SAFETY**

The glass bricks need to be protected during transportation.

## YOU WILL NEED

**Materials** *for a glass waterfall 720 mm high and 1.84 m square*
- Sump: a preformed plastic liner about 660 mm in diameter, with a lid to fit
- Plastic sheet: about 1.5 m square
- Medium-size submersible pump
- Flexible armoured plastic pipe: long enough to protect the full length of pump cable
- Electricity circuit breaker
- Concrete slabs: 9 concrete slabs – 1 x 600 mm square, and 8 x 460 mm square
- Waterproof tile cement, as used in bathrooms and swimming pools: 10 kg
- Glass bricks: 6 x 240 mm-square glass bricks, 80 mm thick
- Soft, pliable copper pipe: 1.5 m long and 10 mm in diameter (as used by gas fitters)
- Copper T-junction: pre-soldered junction to fit the 10 mm tube
- Copper sheet: 500 mm long, 160 mm wide, 1 mm thick
- Flexible galvanized wire cable: 5 m long and about 2 mm in diameter (as sold by yacht chandlers)

- Plastic tube: 500 mm long and 10 mm in diameter (to link the copper tube to the pump), with hose clips to fit
- Rafter nail for toggle: 100 mm long
- Oyster shell: 25 kg washed shell
- Woodchips: 5 wheelbarrow loads

**Tools**
- Wheelbarrow
- Spade
- Scissors
- Straight-edge and chalk
- Electric drill with a 10 mm masonry bit
- Pointing trowel
- Sponge
- Pipe cutter: a plumber's pipe cutter large enough to cut the 10 mm pipe
- Blowlamp: plumber's gas blowlamp
- Claw hammer
- Hand drill with a 2 mm twist bit
- Metal snips: a pair of metalworker's tin snips large enough to cut the copper sheet
- Mallet
- Piece of wood: 500 mm long, 80 mm thick
- Work table with adjustable clamps
- Spirit level

CROSS-SECTION SIDE VIEW OF THE GLASS WATERFALL

Copper water pipe *Connected to the pump*

Drilled copper pipe

Tension wires

Copper sleeve

Glass brick

Large paving slab *drilled for tension wires and copper pipe*

Tension wires *Joined and fixed to underside of paver*

Soil

Plastic sheet

Buried armoured pipe *Protects power cable*

Moulded plastic sump

Pump

Water

## THE MAGIC OF GLASS

Glass bricks are actually as strong as house bricks, but glass itself is potentially a very dangerous material. So, if you have boisterous children or pets, or you are in any way worried about safety, it may be better to select another project.

The bricks are cemented together as two three-brick towers, with the bottoms cushioned in cement, the tops clenched by a copper sleeve, and the whole construction triangulated and held taut by yacht rigging cable. The structure is surprisingly strong and flexible – a bit like a mast. While you are putting it together, it is essential to make sure that the bottoms of the glass bricks cannot slide out of alignment on the slab – if you get that right, the rest is comparatively easy. The other thing to bear in mind, when you look at the step-by-step photographs, is that the overall effect will be enhanced when the copper weathers and turns green.

# Glass waterfall

## PLAN VIEW OF PAVERS

Small paving slab
*460 x 460 mm*

Oyster shell
*Covers central area*

Area of bucket
part of sump

Woodchips
*Cover outer area*

Large paving slab
*600 x 600 mm*
*Hole drilled in centre, and*
*100 mm in from each end*
*of a diagonal running through*
*the centre to the corners*

Moulded plastic
outer ledge of sump

Edge of plastic sheet
*Held in place by pavers*

## PATTERN FOR COPPER SLEEVE

*500 mm*

40 mm

80 mm

40 mm

Rounded corners

Fold lines

Notches to hold tension wires

Drilled hole for water pipe

## FRONT VIEW OF THE GLASS WATERFALL

250 mm x 10 mm
(finished length)

T-junction joint

250 mm x 10 mm
(finished length)

**Copper sleeve
(partially drawn)**
A tight push-fit
over the top of the
glass bricks

**Pipe ends**
Sealed by
hammering over

**Copper "T" crossbar**
Soft copper pipe
with holes drilled on
the underside

**Joint**
Fixed with waterproof
tile cement

**Glass brick**
240 x 240 x 80 mm
Colour and texture to suit

**Copper "T" upright**
800 mm x 10 mm
Soft copper pipe with holes
drilled on the underside

Oyster shell

Large paving slab

Hole drilled in paver

**Toggle**
Tension wire fixed on underside of
paver with a toggle (100 mm nail)

## DETAIL OF T-JUNCTION

**T-junction joint**
Either soldered or compression

**Pipe ends**
Flattened, bent
and sealed

**Notch**
Cut in copper sleeve to
hold tension wires in place

**Tension wires**
Looped around central copper
upright pipe for water feed

**Holes**
Copper pipe with holes
drilled to create waterfall

**Glass bricks**

## Step-by-step: Making the glass waterfall

*Plastic sheet*
*Cut the liner so that it covers the brim of the sump*

*Drilling holes*
*Let the drill bit do the work and do not use excessive force*

*Pump*
*Test the pump after every fitting stage*

*Getting started*
*If your paver seems extra tough, it may be easier to drill a starter hole with a small-diameter drill bit*

*Safety*
*The drilling creates a lot of dust, so wear goggles and a dust-mask*

**1** Dig a hole large enough for the sump. Cover the sump with the plastic sheet, and cut and shape the sheet with scissors so that all the water runs back into the sump. Fit the pump, together with the armoured cable and electricity circuit breaker (see page 54, step 2).

**2** Find the centre of the large concrete slab by drawing diagonals with the chalk and the straight-edge. Use the electric drill and the 10 mm bit to run three holes through the slab — one at the centre, and the other two about 100 mm in from the corners.

*Alignment*
*Check the bricks are aligned with each other and each column is vertical*

*Cleaning the joints*
*Wipe away the excess tile cement to achieve the best possible finish*

**3** Mix the tile cement to a very firm consistency with water, then use the pointing trowel to build the glass bricks into two towers, three bricks high. Sponge the excess cement off the face of the glass.

### *Helpful hint*

If you want to take this project further and build a larger wall — higher than three blocks — you will need to reinforce the wall, either by enclosing it with a metal frame, or by building the glass blocks into a traditional brick wall.

*Drilling*
*Be careful not to drill right through the pipe*

*Mallet*
*Ideally you need to use a heavyweight mallet*

*Sealed ends*
*Fold the ends of the pipe over twice to make them watertight*

*Wood*
*Use the piece of wood to form the copper shape*

*Hardening*
*After shaping, the copper will become more springy, which will help it grip the glass bricks*

**4** To make the copper "T", cut the copper pipe into three pieces with the pipe cutter, slide them into the T-junction, and solder the joint with the blowlamp. Flatten and roll the top ends of the "T" with the claw hammer, and use the hand drill and the 2 mm bit to drill the spray holes on the underside of the arms.

**5** To make the copper sleeve, cut the copper sheet to size with the metal snips, soften it with the blowlamp, and use the mallet to fold it round the piece of wood, so that the resulting sleeve is a tight push-fit over the glass bricks.

*Tension wire*
*Adjust the wire at the top point so that the glass bricks arc at 90° to the concrete slab*

**6** Cement the two glass towers in place on the slab (they should be almost touching). Sit the arrangement on the work table and run the galvanized cable up from the underside through a corner hole in the slab, feeding it up and around the neck of the copper "T", back down the same corner hole, then across to the other corner hole. Repeat the process from that side. Tighten the wire by twisting the ends together on the underside of the slab, using the nail toggle.

Set the structure in place over the sump, check the level with the spirit level and using the plastic tube, link up with the pump. Decorate the arrangement with the smaller concrete slabs and the oyster shell. Spread woodchips around the perimeter.

# Still pond

This pond is reminiscent of Italian courtyards. It can be built with the minimum of effort – there is no digging involved, no cement to mix, and no concrete slabs to cut. Instead it uses various sizes of paving slab, bedded on a layer of raked shingle. The pond is created in a wooden frame. The design of the still pond is such that it can be swiftly remodelled at a later date if you want a change.

### TIME

A weekend (eight hours for building the wooden frame and setting it in the bed of shingle, and eight hours for arranging the slabs).

### SAFETY

Always keep an eye on children playing near a pond, just in case the slabs tip up and move. If you have very young children, it may be better not to have a pond.

## CROSS-SECTION OF THE STILL POND

Floating plant
To help shade areas of the pond from sun

Oxygenating plant
To keep the water clear

Large paver

Wooden frame
Pre-treated with preservative

Woven plastic

Brick
Positioned to support overhanging paving slab

Plastic liner

Soil

Shingle
Compacted and levelled

## YOU WILL NEED

**Materials** *for a pond 2.6 m long and 1.4 m wide*
- Weed-stop plastic sheet: as large as your site
- Shingle (medium): 1 tonne washed shingle
- Wood: 3 x 2.44 m lengths of 100 mm square-section sawn and treated softwood
- Nails: 4 x 150 mm long
- Sand: 2 wheelbarrow loads
- Plastic sheet: 3 m long and 1.8 m wide

- Concrete paving slabs: 20 in various sizes, shapes and colours, ranging from small 300 mm squares through to large 450 mm squares, plus lozenges and rectangles
- Bricks: 8 house bricks

**Tools**
- Wheelbarrow
- Shovel
- Rake
- Spirit level
- Tape measure and a pencil
- Crosscut saw
- Claw hammer

## A RING OF STILL WATER

The clever thing about this project is the fact that it can be completed with just about any shape of slab that comes to hand, without the need to cut to fit. At first sight the pattern of slabs might look a little complicated, but basically there are two lines of slabs, one at each side of the pond. As long as the lines extend a bit further than the length of the pond, the sequence or shape of the slabs is not important. The slabs that extend into the body of the water are supported by little stacks of bricks, rather like mini piers. It is best to avoid walking on the extended slabs, just in case they wobble or break under your weight.

There are two ways of looking at this project. It can either be seen as a temporary eye-catcher – the sort of feature that you build to occupy a space that is waiting for something else to come along and fill it, or you simply enjoy changing the design as and when you feel like it. The unique feature of this design is that you do not need to plan out the arrangement of the slabs – you just start at one end of the pond and finish at the other, working according to materials and inspiration.

# Still pond

**Wooden frame**
*Sides 2.44 m long, ends 1.22 m long. Made from pre-treated wood*

**Oxygenating plants**
*Chosen for their water-freshening qualities*

**Floating plants**
*Help minimize the growth of algae*

**Water**

**Shingle**
*Raked level with the slabs*

**Paving slab**
*Overlaps pond to create interesting patterns and shapes*

**Island paver**
*Supported by several bricks*

**Paving slabs**
Different shaped pavers create an interesting design

**Marginal plant**
In container basket

**Plastic sheet**
Laps over the wooden frame

**Wooden frame**
Bedded and levelled on the shingle

**Corners**
Frame fixed with crossed nails

**Soil**

**Supporting bricks**
Placed under extended slabs

**Sand**
Levelled within the wooden frame

**Strong woven plastic**
To keep down weeds

# Step-by-step: Making the still pond

*Shingle*
*Rake the shingle level*

*Weed-stop
plastic sheet*
*Use woven
plastic sheet
to prevent
weeds while
permitting
drainage*

*Shingle*
*Rake the surrounding shingle
level with the top of the frame*

*Levelling*
*Test to see if
the frame is
level and make
any necessary
adjustments*

*Sand*
*After levelling
the shingle,
spread a layer
of sand over it*

**1** Spread the weed-stop plastic sheet over the whole site and cover it with a good layer of raked shingle. Check that all is level with the spirit level.

**2** Build the wooden frame with the saw, hammer and nails, and place it on the levelled shingle. Spread a bed of sand inside the frame and rake it over the shingle to a depth of about 80 mm.

*Plastic sheet*
*Spread the edge of the plastic sheet
over the top of the wooden frame*

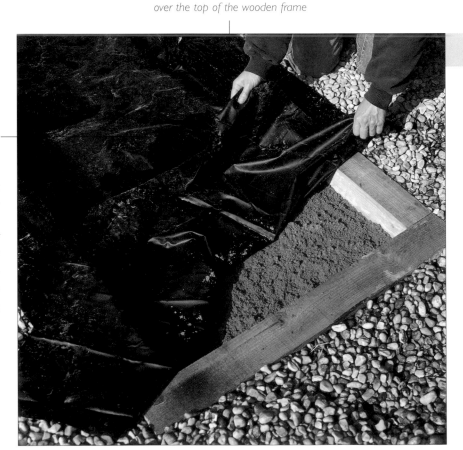

*Wrinkles*
*When you have
arranged the
plastic as best
you can, pour
in a little water.
The weight of
the water will
indicate any
tight or
slack areas*

**3** Spread the plastic sheet over both the frame and the sand, to form the pond liner. Fill the pond with water and cover the edge of the plastic with shingle, so that the top edge of the frame and the surrounding shingle are all at the same level.

### Helpful hint

If you want to make this a more permanent structure, simply lay a concrete slab foundation, replace the wooden edging with a mini wall of concrete blocks or bricks bedded in mortar, and then follow on with the sand and the plastic sheet as described.

*Handling the slabs*
*Lower the slabs gently so that*
*you don't damage the plastic*

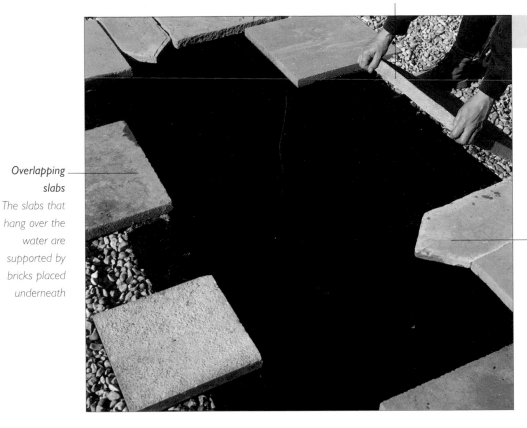

**4** Lay the concrete slabs in place around the pond. Arrange selected slabs so that they extend into the water, supporting them with carefully arranged groups of bricks. Make sure that all the slabs are stable enough to support your weight.

*Overlapping*
*slabs*
*The slabs that hang over the water are supported by bricks placed underneath*

*Experimentation*
*Try out different arrangements of slabs until you find one that you prefer*

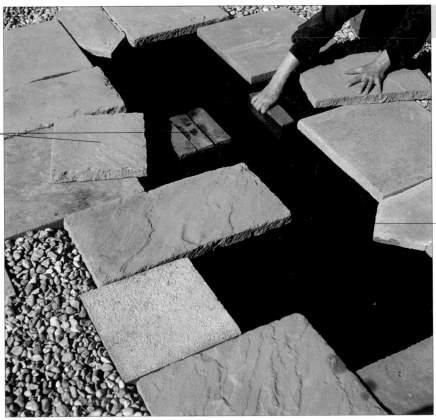

**5** Once you have finalized your arrangement of slabs, spend time checking that the overhanging slabs are adequately supported by the bricks — use more bricks if necessary. Sit pots of oxygenating plants in the water and for the finishing touch, place container plants on the slabs and the surrounding shingle.

*"Island"*
*Build a brick and slab island in the middle of the pond*

*Pond shape*
*The shape of the water is as important as the pattern of slabs — you may want both to be regular and less random*

# Rocky cascade

The rocky cascade was inspired by a beautiful mountain spring that we saw in the wilds of Wales. Icy water pushed up out of the hillside and cascaded down a series of rocky steps into a huge basin below. The whole vision was one of movement and sound, with water running, flowing, gushing, smashing, trickling and dripping over the stone. This project recreates the scene in miniature.

**TIME**

Four weekends (two days to dig the terrace, two days to sort out the plastic sheet, fit the pump and build the first wall, and the other four days for finishing the stonework).

**SAFETY**

This project involves a lot of physical work so, if possible, get someone to help you.

## YOU WILL NEED

**Materials** *for a cascade 1.4 m high, 3 m long and 3 m wide*

- Soil: 3 tonnes soil (this could be the spoil pile dug when building a pond – see the Natural Pond on page 118)
- Submersible pump: largest pump that you can afford
- Flexible armoured plastic pipe: long enough to protect the full length of the pump cable and filter cable
- Electricity circuit breaker
- Filtration system to fit your pump: biggest system you can afford
- Plastic water delivery pipe: 6 m long, 35 mm in diameter (best-quality ribbed pipe with connectors to fit your pump and filtration system)
- Sand: 250 kg soft sand
- Butyl pond liner: best-quality liner, 3.6 m long, 1.8 m wide, 1 mm thick

- Mortar: 2 parts (200 kg) cement, 1 part (100 kg) lime, 9 parts (900 kg) soft sand
- Split sandstone: approximately 3 cubic metres (for the various steps and ledges)
- Secondary rocks: 1 tonne medium-sized sandstone rocks
- Shingle (medium to large): 1 tonne washed shingle
- Alpine grit: 75 kg crushed granite
- Cobbles: 150 kg large cobbles
- Feature rocks: 3 tonnes large sandstone rocks – as large as you can move

**Tools**
- Wheelbarrow
- Spade
- Shovel
- Spirit level
- Pointing trowel
- Mason's hammer
- Garden hose

## A FLIGHT OF WATER

Of all the projects in the book, this is the most stunning, the most expensive, the most time-consuming, and the most rewarding. Earth has to be piled up and sculpted, rocks have to be heaved about the garden, and of course, if you do not already have a pond, you have to build one. (Follow the instructions for the large Natural Pond on page 118, and then simply use the spoil from the hole to create the mound that is the basis of the cascade.)

This project cannot be rushed, so be prepared for it to take up a lot of your time. Also, the only way to move a significant amount of water from the pond to the top of the mound is to invest in a large pump. Despite all these things, the rocky cascade is great to watch in action – well worth all the effort involved!

### CROSS-SECTION OF THE ROCKY CASCADE

Stone slabs

Thick pond liner

Raised ledge
*To allow water to flow underneath*

Water

Large pump

Brick support

Plastic water delivery pipe
*Takes water to the top of the cascade. It is buried in the flower border (or rockery) beside the cascade*

Soil

Buried armoured pipe
*Protecting the power cable from damage*

Filter
*Concealed in the flower border (or rockery)*

# Rocky cascade

FRONT VIEW OF THE ROCKY CASCADE

**Cascade**
Constructed out
of courses of
split sandstone

**Water delivery pipe**
Hidden by large piece
of split sandstone

**Retaining wall**
Forms steps for
the cascade

**Water delivery pipe**
Buried in rockery

**Shallow pool**

**Filter**
Partly buried

**Stone edge of pond**
Lapped over the edge
of the butyl liner

**Large sandstone feature rocks
and medium-sized secondary rocks**
Placed around the cascade

**Small piece
of split sandstone**
Placed to divert
water flow

**Large pump**
Sits on bricks to keep
it clear of sludge

**Grass edge to pond**
Created with turf

**Buried armoured pipe**
Protects the power cable

PLAN VIEW OF THE ROCKY CASCADE

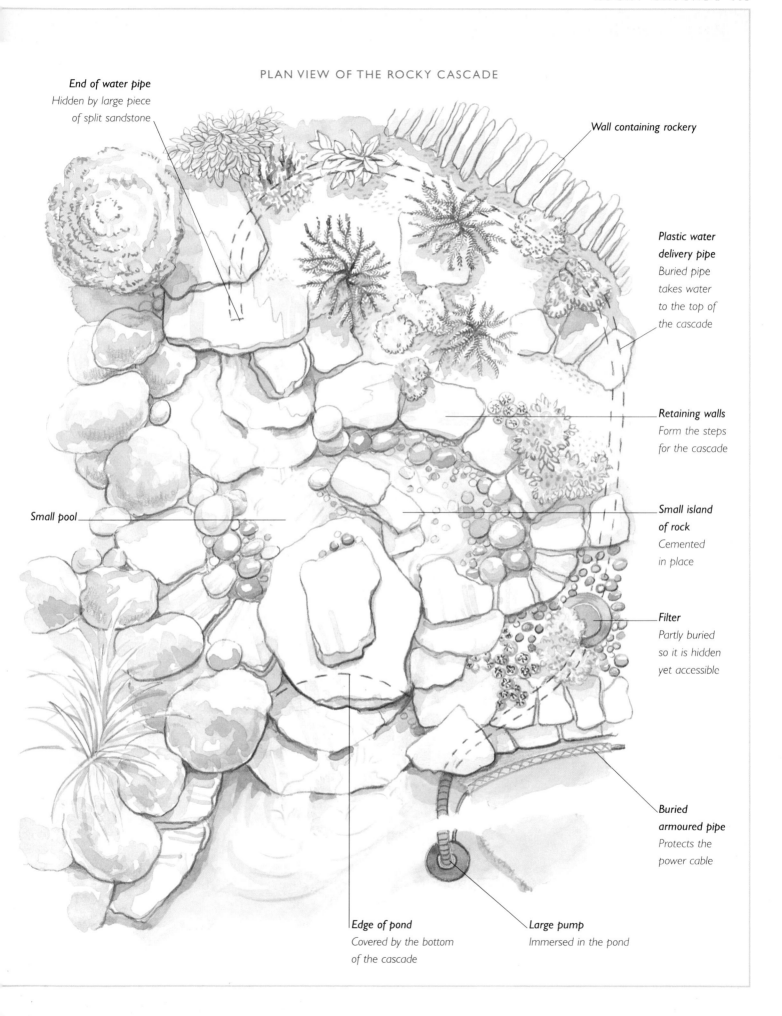

**End of water pipe**
*Hidden by large piece
of split sandstone*

**Wall containing rockery**

**Plastic water
delivery pipe**
*Buried pipe
takes water
to the top of
the cascade*

**Retaining walls**
*Form the steps
for the cascade*

**Small pool**

**Small island
of rock**
*Cemented
in place*

**Filter**
*Partly buried
so it is hidden
yet accessible*

**Buried
armoured pipe**
*Protects the
power cable*

**Edge of pond**
*Covered by the bottom
of the cascade*

**Large pump**
*Immersed in the pond*

## Step-by-step: Making the rocky cascade

*Steps*
*Use the spade to sculpt straight-sided steps in the earth*

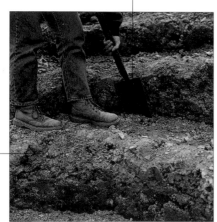

*Water delivery pipe*
*We specify 35 mm pipe, but choose pipe to suit your pump model*

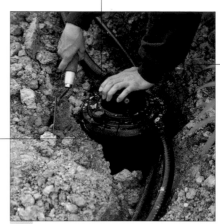

*Preserving the edges*
*Avoid standing on the edges of the steps*

*Filling in*
*Push sand and earth around the sides of the filtration unit*

*Access*
*Follow the manufacturer's instructions for leaving room for access to the filtration unit, for maintenance*

**1** Build the mound of earth for the cascade alongside your pond. Use the spade and shovel to cut a series of steps that run from the top of the mound down into the pond. Check that they are horizontal with the spirit level.

**2** Set the pump in the water complete with the armoured pipe, electricity circuit breaker and plastic water delivery pipe. Bury all the pipes and the bottom half of the filtration plant.

*Following the steps*
*Let the liner fall into the shape of the steps*

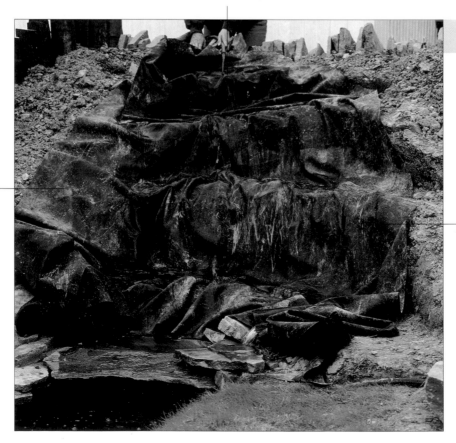

**3** Cover the whole stepped face of the mound with sand, then carefully lay the butyl liner over it. Using the pointing trowel, build the bottom step with the spilt sandstone and mortar. Lap the lower edge of the liner over the bottom step.

*High-quality butyl pond liner*
*Buy the best thick liner that you can afford*

*Positioning*
*Working from all sides, drag the sheet into place*

*Body weight*
*Keep your feet well away from the wall*

*Split sandstone slab*
*Choose a large slab for the base of the cascade*

*Water flow*
*Use a hosepipe to test how the water will flow*

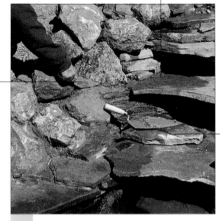

*Secondary slabs*
*Place smaller slabs to divert the flow of the water*

*Mortar*
*Force mortar into all the joints and small cavities*

**4** Build a low wall of split sandstone and mortar at the back of the bottom step, using the pointing trowel and the mason's hammer. This holds the butyl liner in place and forms the riser for the next step. Pack earth and rubble behind the wall.

**5** Continue building walls and steps until you reach the top of the mound. At intervals during the process (and when the mortar has begun to set), use a garden hose to check how the water flows from one step to another. If necessary, make adjustments and block gaps with extra stone and mortar.

*Water flow*
*Moving a rock slightly can change the water flow*

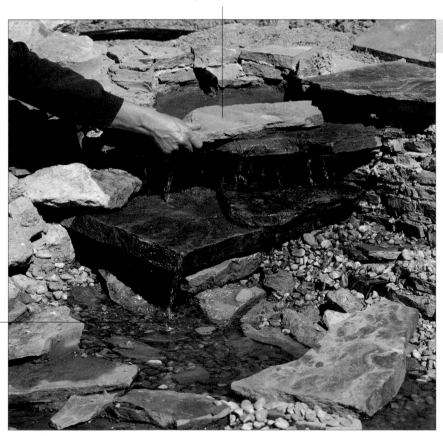

*Rock pools*
*Pools of water look good and improve the sound of the cascade*

**6** Finally, when the mortar has completely cured, use the secondary rocks, shingle, alpine grit and cobbles to fill and embellish selected pools and steps. Place large feature rocks on the steps to create extra runs and eddies.

### Helpful hint

Within hours of building this project and turning on the pump, we spotted two frogs sitting under one of the overhanging slabs. You too can encourage frogs to take up residence by building little nooks and crannies into the structure.

# Natural pond

There is nothing quite so satisfying as a natural pond. The ever-changing character of the water, the host of plants and, of course, the abundant wildlife – frogs leaping, bugs scudding across the surface of the water, dragonflies hovering – all come together to create a uniquely beautiful balance of nature.

CROSS-SECTION OF
THE NATURAL POND

*Boulders*
*Heavy rocks hold*
*slabs in place*

*Sandstone slabs*

*Marginal plant*
*Steps built for*
*shallow-water plants*

*Water lily*
*Water lilies like*
*deep, still water*

*Floating plant*

*Underlay*
*Loft insulation protects*
*the liner from sharp*
*objects and covers*
*near-vertical sides*

*Oxygenating plant*

*Sand*
*Sand protects the liner*

*Pond liner*
*1 mm thick*

*Bog area*
*An area of wet, marshy soil*
*where bog plants will thrive*

## YOU WILL NEED

**Materials** *for a pond 5 m long and 1.7 m wide, with a maximum depth of 500 mm*
• Sand: 500 kg soft sand
• Loft insulation: 2 x 9.17 m rolls of glass wool, 600 mm wide and 50 mm thick
• Butyl pond liner: best-quality liner, 9.6 m long, 3.6 m wide, 1 mm thick
• Turf: 4 rolls, 1.5 m long and about 40 mm wide
• Split sandstone: 4 square metres
• Mortar: 2 parts (100 kg) cement, 1 part (50 kg) lime, 9 parts (450 kg) soft sand
• Limestone: 12 basketball-sized boulders

• Grit for base of bog garden: 1 bucketful

**Tools**
• Wheelbarrow
• Bucket
• Length of rope
• Tape measure
• Spade
• Shovel
• Spirit level
• Batten (wide enough to span your pond)
• Lawn rake
• Heavy-duty scissors
• Club hammer
• Bricklayer's trowel
• Pointing trowel

## LIVING WATER

The pond is constructed with steps at various levels. Starting at the edge of the pond, there is a step for the edge of the liner flap, a step for marginal plants, and a gentle slope down to the bottom of the pond. At one side of the pond, the edge of the liner is held down by a mixture of flat slabs of sandstone and limestone boulders, while at the other side it runs under a bank of turf and stones, then on into a slow-draining bog garden ditch.

To protect the butyl liner from being pierced by sharp stones, there is a layer of soft sand over most of the horizontal areas and a layer of glass wool loft insulation over the vertical risers. We opted for a layer of glass wool because our soil is very stony. If your soil is soft and sandy, you could use polyester underlay.

Plan the planting carefully. You need oxygenating plants to keep the water clear, several showy specimen plants for deep-water areas (such as water lilies), marginal plants for the shallow steps around the edges of the pond, and bog plants for the bog areas. If there are bog plants in other parts of the garden, lift, divide and replant them around the pond. If you get the balance of plants right, the water will have cleared about three weeks after planting.

# Natural pond

PLAN VIEW OF THE NATURAL POND

**Limestone boulders**
*Mortared on to slabs*

**Floating plants**

**Oxygenating plants**
*Help maintain balance of the pond*

**Sandstone slabs**
*Cover liner and hold it in place*

**Shelf**
*For marginal plants*

**Turf**
*Two layers of turf are used to create grass edges*

**Butyl liner**
*Overhangs edge of pond*

**Small slabs of stone**
*Disguise the step used for marginal plants*

**Rockery**
*On sloping side of pond*

**Rocks**
*Bedded in mortar*

**Bog plants**

**Butyl liner**

**Rich organic soil**

**Grit**
*Spread in bottom of ditch*

**Drainage holes**
*In butyl liner to bog area*

**Small ditch**
*Forms the bog area*

**Loft insulation**
*Covers the sides*

**Soil**

**Excavated width of pond**
*1.7 m*

**Marginal plant**

**Deep-water plant**

**Sand**

## Step-by-step: Making the natural pond

*Earth pile*
*Push the spoil away so that it doesn't fall back*

*Edges*
*Sculpt the edges to a good finish*

*Levelling*
*The pond edges need to be perfectly level*

*Stones*
*Remove all the sharp stones*

*Sand*
*Rake the sand into a smooth layer, removing protruding stones as you work*

**1** Mark out the overall shape of the pond with rope and the tape measure, and use the spade and the shovel to dig out the earth to the desired depth. With the spirit level and batten, check that the pond edges are all at the same level.

**2** Remove all sticks and stones, then spread and rake a bed of soft sand over the entire base of the pond (include all horizontal surfaces). Aim for an overall thickness of no less than 80 mm.

*Bank*
*The bank needs to be sufficiently wide to support the slabs and boulders that make up the edge*

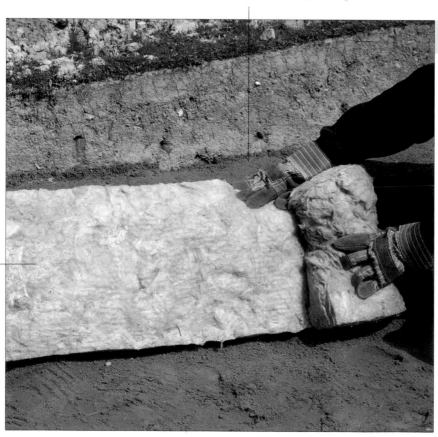

*Loft insulation*
*The insulation material can cause skin irritation. Wear gloves and tuck your sleeves into them*

**3** To prevent stones piercing the liner, cover all vertical surfaces with the loft insulation (cut it to shape with the scissors). Continue adding sand and loft insulation until you are sure all sharp edges are covered to a good depth.

### Helpful hint

If the weather is at all windy, the loft insulation may blow about the garden. Do not unroll it until the very last moment (just minutes before laying the plastic sheet). Alternatively, dip it into water so that it is a sodden mass that is unlikely to blow away.

*Liner*
*Take your time arranging the butyl liner, so that*
*you have equal amounts overlapping all round*

*Arranging the turf*
*Lay a layer of turf with the earth side up,*
*followed by a layer with the grass side up*

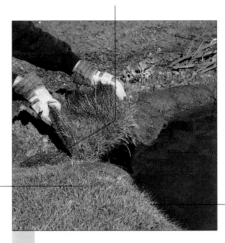

*Water*
*Fill the pond*
*with a little*
*water – its*
*weight will*
*indicate where*
*the liner needs*
*rearranging*

*Watering*
*Keep the turf*
*well watered*
*until it is*
*established*

*Water level*
*Let the edges*
*of the turf trail*
*in the water*

**4** Being very careful not to dig holes in the sand or dislodge the loft insulation, gently unroll the butyl liner over the whole pond. Slowly fill the pond with water, all the while easing and gently smoothing the rubber to avoid thick folds.

**5** Cover selected edges of the pond with sandwiched turf. Lay the first layer of turf with the earth side uppermost, and then top it off with a layer placed with the grass side uppermost. This will grow together into a compacted mat that covers the liner and edges the pond.

*Firmly fixed boulders*
*Use plenty of mortar to*
*secure the boulders*

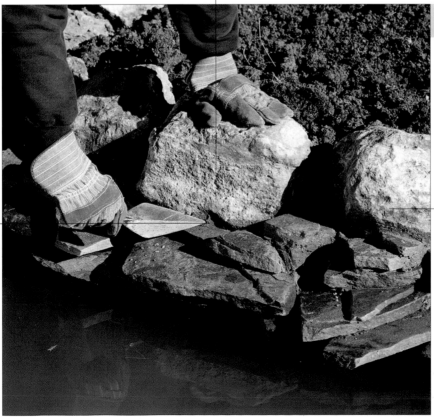

*Mortar*
*Scrape away*
*and reshape*
*the mortar*
*joints until they*
*look good*

**6** When you come to the stone edging, first bed the split sandstone in the mortar, using the club hammer and the two trowels, then top it off with limestone boulders and mortar. Add additional courses of stone and mortar to suit the levels of your particular pond.

*Work carefully*
*Remember that*
*pond liners are*
*fragile, so when you*
*are moving stones*
*be extra careful not*
*to let them fall in*
*the pond*

## Inspirations: Natural ponds

**The creation of a healthy, natural pond involves bringing together a complex mix of water, plants, bugs, bacteria and animals, to create a well-balanced whole. The animals use oxygen and give out carbon dioxide, the plants absorb carbon dioxide and give out oxygen, the animals eat the plants, the plants and bacteria absorb sunlight – and so the eco-circle keeps turning.**

ABOVE **A raised formal courtyard pond, built out of brick and edged with concrete slabs. This could be described as a "natural" pond, in the sense that** it provides a suitable environment for plants and animals. If a pond can be maintained without the need for fountains and filters, it is natural. When stocking a pond with plants, do it in stages, so the individual plants gradually acclimatize to the water temperature and each other.

ABOVE AND LEFT **A beautiful example of a natural pond. Bright, clear water, thriving plants, the presence of fish, frogs, gnats, water snails and dragonflies, all suggest that the ecosystem of the pond is well balanced. If you can look down into the water and see colonies of animals and plants, you can be sure that the pond is healthy.**

# Glossary

**Aggregate** A mix of sand and crushed stone used with cement to make concrete.

**Algae** Minute, non-flowering water plant – resembles a film of green slime on the water surface.

**Aquatic** A general term for plants that thrive in water, or in waterlogged soil.

**Bog garden** An area – in a container or garden – where the soil is permanently wet.

**Circuit breaker** Also called a residual current device (RCD) – an automatic cut-out – used in conjunction with electrical pumps and tools as a safety measure.

**Delivery pipe** The pipe that runs from the delivery side of the pump – the pipe from which the water flows.

**Filter** A piece of foam in a submersible pump that filters mud, grit and algae from water. A filtration unit (connected to a pump) for cleaning water.

**Flexible armoured pipe** A heavy-duty pipe used to protect a power cable.

**Flexible liner** A sheet of reinforced rubber or thick plastic used for waterproofing ponds and other water features.

**Hardcore** Broken stone, brick or builder's rubble used to create a firm base.

**Levelling** Using a spirit level to decide whether or not a structure is level and then going on to make the necessary adjustments.

**Log roll** Edging made from logs and wire – good for edging borders and water features.

**Marking out** Using a string, pegs, and tape measure to set out the size of the project on the ground.

**Oxygenator** A water plant that releases oxygen into the water.

**Pea gravel** A fine pea-sized gravel used as a decorative feature or as a levelling layer.

**Pre-formed unit** A factory-made concrete or plastic moulding – it might be a whole pond, a sump, or part of a waterfall.

**Reservoir pool** A pool or tank of water at the lowest point of the feature – the pool in which the pump sits.

**Rubber matting** A sheet of thick rubber used to protect the pond liner – from a heavy block or slab, for example.

**Sealant** A soft plastic or liquid compound used as a waterproofing material – for holes, seams, and porous surfaces.

**Sighting** To judge by eye, or to look at the feature in order to determine whether or not the structure is level.

**Siting** Deciding whereabouts on the site – in the garden or on the plot – the water feature is going to be placed.

**Submersible pump** A pump that is positioned underwater.

**Sump** A small pond or pool into which the water drains – the pool that contains the pump.

**Underlay** A cushioning layer underneath the liner used as a protection from sharp stones – it could be a specialist pond underlay or roof insulation.

# Suppliers

**UK**

*Consult the telephone directory for details of your local water garden specialist and DIY store.*

Blagdon Water Gardens
Bath Road
Upper Langford
Somerset
BS18 7DN
Tel: (01934) 852973

Hozelock Ltd
Waterslade House
Thame Road
Haddenham
Aylesbury
Buckinghamshire
HP17 8JD
Tel: (01844) 291881

Interpet
Interpet House
Vincent Lane
Dorking
Surrey
RH4 3YX
Tel: (01306) 881033

Lotus Water Garden Products
Junction Street
Burnley
Lancashire
BB12 0NA
Tel: (01282) 420771
Fax: (01282) 412719
(Manufacturers of self-contained water features and fountain ornaments)

Oases
3 Telford Gate
Whittle Road
West Portway Industrial Estate
Andover
Hampshire
SP10 3SF
Tel: (01264) 333225
(Pumps)

The Traditional Garden
Supply Co
Scotts of Stowe
Unit 1, Corinium Centre
Lovelane Ind. Estate
Cirencester
Gloucestershire
GL7 1YJ
Orderline: (0870) 600 3366

Trident Water Garden Products
Folehill
Coventry
Warwickshire
CV6 7FL
Tel: (01203) 638802

**SOUTH AFRICA**

*Consult the telephone directory for details of your local water garden specialist and DIY store.*

Dunrobin Garden Pavilion
Old Main Road
Bothas Hill, Durban
Tel: (031) 777 1855
Fax: (031) 777 1893

Lifestyle Garden Centre
DF Malan Drive
Randpark Ridge
Northcliff
Johannesburg
Tel: (011) 792 5616
Fax: (011) 792 5332

Radermachers Garden
and Home Centre
Kraaibosch
National Road
George
Tel: (044) 889 0075/6
Fax: (044) 889 0071

Safari Garden Centre
Lynwood Road
Pretoria
Tel: (012) 807 0009
Fax: (012) 807 0350

Showgrounds Nursery
Showgrounds
Currie Avenue
Bloemfontein
Tel: (051) 447 5523
Fax: (051) 447 5523

Starke Ayres (Pty) Ltd
322 Kempston Road
Sydwill
Port Elizabeth
Tel: (041) 451 0389
Fax: (041) 451 0393
and

Liesbeek Road
Rosebank
Cape Town
Tel: (021) 685 4120
Fax: (021) 685 3837
(Branches nationwide)

**AUSTRALIA**

ABC Timbers and Building
Supplies Pty Ltd
46 Auburn Road
Regents Park
NSW 2143
Tel: (02) 9645 2511

BBC Hardware
Building A
Cnr. Cambridge and
Chester Streets
Epping
NSW 2121
Tel: (02) 9876 0888
(Branches throughout Australia)

Bowens Timber and
Building Supplies
135–173 Macaulay Road
North Melbourne 3051
Tel: (03) 9328 1041

Mitre 10
319 George Street
Sydney 2000
Tel: (02) 9262 1435
Customer service: 1800 777 850
(Outlets nationwide)

Garden Magic
Harrington Park
Cnr. Northern Road and
Porrende Street
Narellan
NSW 2567
Tel: (02) 4647 4332

Above the Earth
70 Ben Boyd Road
Neutral Bay
NSW 2089
(02) 9904 0577
(Design and installation of
ponds, fountains and other
water features; can source any
materials required)

Fantasy Fountains
Unit 2/8 Auburn Street
Hunters Hill
NSW 2110
(02) 9651 1154
(Outlets nationwide)

Garden Art Fountains
269 Parramatta Road (cnr.
Wolseley Street)
Haberfield
NSW 2045

Bambuzit
13 Erith Street
Botany
NSW 2019
(02) 9666 5703
(Bamboo supplier)

**NEW ZEALAND**

Firth Industries Ltd
Auckland Regional Office
102 Lunn Ave
Mt Wellington
Auckland
Information Freephone:
0800 800 576
(Branches nationwide)

Carine Garden Centre and
Water World
Cnr. SH2 and Te Karaka Drive
Te Puna
Tauranga
Tel: (07) 552 4949

Jansen's Pet and Aquatic Centre
985 Mt Eden Road
Three Kings
Auckland
Tel: (09) 625 7915
Website: www.jansens.co.nz

Palmers Garden Centres
Head Office:
182 Wairau Road
Glenfield
Auckland
Tel: (09) 443 9910
(Branches nationwide)

Placemakers Support Office
150 Marua Road
Private Bag 14942
Panmure
Auckland
Tel: (09) 525 5100

# Conversion chart

To convert the metric measurements given in this book to imperial measurements, simply multiply the figure given in the text by the relevant number shown in the table below. Bear in mind that conversions will not necessarily work out exactly, and you will need to round the figure up or down slightly. (Do not use a combination of metric and imperial measurements – for accuracy, keep to one system.)

| To convert | Multiply by |
| --- | --- |
| millimetres to inches | 0.0394 |
| metres to feet | 3.28 |
| metres to yards | 1.093 |
| sq millimetres to sq inches | 0.00155 |
| sq metres to sq feet | 10.76 |
| sq metres to sq yards | 1.195 |
| cu metres to cu feet | 35.31 |
| cu metres to cu yards | 1.308 |
| grams to pounds | 0.0022 |
| kilograms to pounds | 2.2046 |
| litres to gallons | 0.22 |

# Index

### Acknowledgments

AG&G Books would like to thank the following picture libraries for their contribution: *Dennis Davis Photography Design* (page 42 right); *Garden and Wildlife Matters* (page 74 right) and *John Glover Photography* (pages 42 left, 43 right and 74 left).